Insects and Spiders

of the World

VOLUME 1
AFRICANIZED BEE – BEE FLY

Marshall Cavendish
New York • London • Toronto • Sydney

Marshall Cavendish
99 White Plains Road
Tarrytown, New York 10591

Website: www.marshallcavendish.com

Library of Congress Cataloging-in-Publication Data
Insects and spiders of the world.
    p.   cm.
    Contents: v. 1. Africanized bee–Bee fly — v. 2. Beetle–Carpet beetle — v. 3. Carrion beetle–Earwig — v. 4. Endangered species–Gyspy moth v. 5. Harvester ant–Leaf-cutting ant — v. 6. Locomotion–Orb-web spider — v. 7. Owlet moth–Scorpion — v. 8. Scorpion fly–Stinkbug — v. 9. Stone fly–Velvet worm — v. 10. Wandering spider–Zorapteran — v. 11. Index.
    ISBN 0-7614-7334-3 (set) — ISBN 0-7614-7335-1 (v. 1) — ISBN 0-7614-7336-X (v. 2) — ISBN 0-7614-7337-8 (v. 3) — ISBN 0-7614-7338-6 (v. 4) — ISBN 0-7614-7339-4 (v. 5) — ISBN 0-7614-7340-8 (v. 6) — ISBN 0-7614-7341-6 (v. 7) — ISBN 0-7614-7342-4 (v. 8) — ISBN 0-7614-7343-2 (v. 9) — ISBN 0-7614-7344-0 (v. 10) — ISBN 0-7614-7345-9 (v. 11)
    1. Insects. 2. Spiders.   I. Marshall Cavendish Corporation.

QL463 .I732 2003
595.7—dc21

                                                                2001028882

ISBN 0-7614-7334-3 (set)
ISBN 0-7614-7335-1 (volume 1)

Printed in Hong Kong

06 05 04 03 02   6 5 4 3 2 1

Brown Partworks Limited
Project Editor: Tom Jackson
Subeditor: Jim Martin
Managing Editor: Bridget Giles
Design: Graham Curd for WDA
Picture Researcher: Helen Simm
Illustrations: Wildlife Art Limited
Graphics: Darren Awuah, Dax Fullbrook, Mark Walker
Indexer: Kay Ollerenshaw

Marshall Cavendish
Editor: Joyce Tavolacci
Editorial Director: Paul Bernabeo

WRITERS
Dr. Robert S. Anderson
Richard Beatty
Dr. Stuart Church
Dr. Douglas C. Currie
Trevor Day
Dr. Arthur V. Evans
Amanda J. Harman
Dr. Rob Houston
Anne K. Jamieson
Becca Law
Professor Steve Marshall
Jamie McDonald
Ben Morgan
Dr. Kieren Pitts
Rebecca Saunders
Dr. Joseph L. Thorley
Dr. Gavin Wilson

COVER: Assassin bug **(Oxford Scientific Films)**
TITLE PAGE: Medfly **(Agricultural Research Service, USDA)**

INTRODUCTION

"Most children have a bug period. I never grew out of mine."

E. O. Wilson, Curator of Entomology, Harvard University

I never outgrew my bug period either. I have always been fascinated by insects and other arthropods. Growing up on the edge of the Mojave Desert in California, I was fortunate to live in a rich and varied habitat full of arthropods of all kinds. Our backyard was an oasis in the middle of the desert. Countless insects, spiders, millipedes, centipedes, and pill bugs sought shelter among the low canopy of creeping ivy and grapevines. They grazed on the grassy plains of our lawn, laid eggs inside the weedy thickets, and hunted among the sweet-smelling lilac hedges.

Season by season
Mourning cloak butterflies announced the first warm days of spring by emerging from their winter hiding places. By tucking themselves away in crevices of bark during the previous fall, these nearly black butterflies, trimmed in yellow, managed to escape the harsh winters of the high desert. Black and red harvester ants toiled in the summer sun like miniature bulldozers, frantically digging underground chambers in the compact desert sands. In these chambers the ants stored all kinds of dried seeds for food. The entrances to their nests were neatly swept by the steady stream of ants entering and leaving. Warm autumn nights were filled with the gentle calls of male katydids seeking mates. These green leafy insects resembled the leaves of the elm trees where they lived.

Feeding the imagination
My parents encouraged my interests in insects. While many moms might have squirmed at the sight of insects, mine kept large Mediterranean mantises inside the house, where they lived on top of the dining-room curtains.

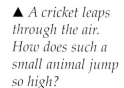

▲ *A cricket leaps through the air. How does such a small animal jump so high?*

▼ *A scorpion mother carries her young on her back. Do any other arthropods do this?*

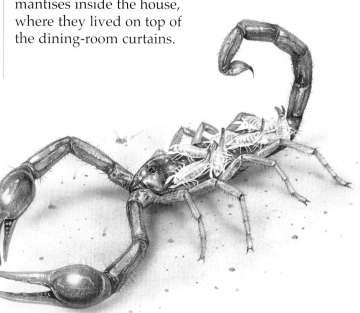

3

▲ *A spitting spider catches a fly with a jet of sticky glue. How do other spiders catch their prey?*

milkweed, where I could observe them more closely. Feeding almost continuously on the bitter leaves, my amazing new pets increased their size thousands of times in just a few weeks before becoming beautiful monarch butterflies.

Still amazed

Even today, many years later, as a scientist, writer, and photographer, I am still in awe of these incredible animals. Arthropods continue to open my eyes to new worlds, fueling my wonder of the natural world and leading me to new and exciting discoveries. *Insects and Spiders of the World* will take readers on a similar journey of discovery, providing the first of many glimpses into a world that is seldom seen and rarely appreciated.

Dr. Arthur V. Evans
Smithsonian Institution,
Washington, D.C.

Everyday, my dad would skewer some flies on a sewing needle, and dangle the wriggling shish kebab by a thread in front of the hungry predators. The mantises would strike out at their dinner, grabbing the needle with spiny legs and nibbling on the stack of impaled insects, as if they were eating an ear of corn. I thought it was much better than going to the zoo.

Small adventures

My search for arthropods took me on many adventures, not unlike safaris in Africa. At night, I would use my flashlight to track cicada nymphs as they left their burrows in the ground to slowly crawl up a tree trunk. Witnessing the transformation of these humpbacked creatures into elegant adult cicadas is one of the great marvels of nature.

On one trip I gathered tiny black, yellow, and white caterpillars to raise in my bedroom on fresh cuttings of

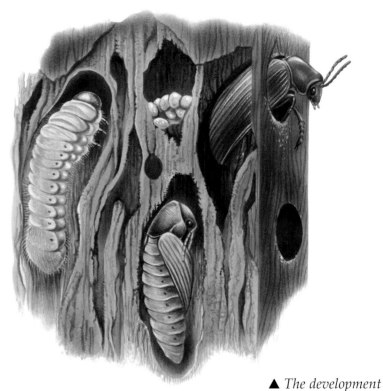

▲ *The development of a furniture beetle. What other insects eat wood?*

READER'S GUIDE

Welcome to *Insects and Spiders of the World.* This page explains how to use these volumes to find out what you want to know. There are nearly 200 articles in the first ten volumes of this set. All articles are arranged alphabetically. To find an article on a particular subject, use the contents list that appears on the next page. If an article is not listed there, try looking up your subject in the index in Volume 11, which includes a comprehensive index for the whole set, as well as several smaller indexes broken down into subjects. Each volume has a contents list and index of its own, and at the back of every book a glossary defines important terms.

All the articles are illustrated with color photographs and artworks. Basic pieces of information are given in the "Key Facts" sections that run down the sides of many pages. Most articles are accompanied by a map that shows where certain insects or spiders live in the world, and many of the longer articles have boxes that focus on special subjects in greater detail. Finally, all the articles contain a "See Also" box, which lists articles elsewhere in the set that are about a related subject.

Every article in this set can be grouped into one of four thematic categories. You can see which category an article belongs to by looking at the color of the heading that runs along the top of each page.

The four categories are Insects, Spiders, Other Arthropods, and Overviews. Articles on particular insects use a green highlight; spider articles use yellow; articles on other arthropods, which include articles on animals that are very closely related to insects and spiders, use red; and overview articles, which cover broad subjects, use blue.

▼ *Check the color of the heading to find out what category an article is in.*

INSECTS

SPIDERS

OTHER ARTHROPODS

OVERVIEW

article title · color bar · introduction · map · category of article

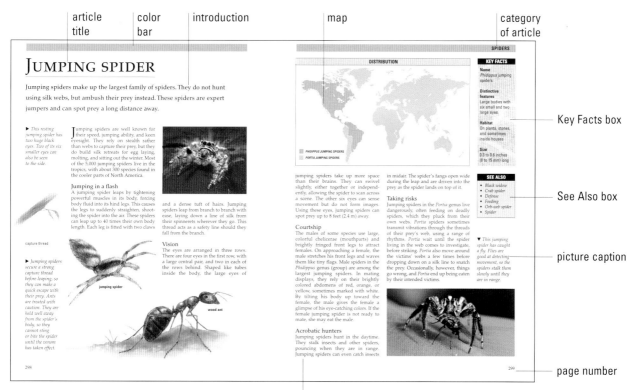

Key Facts box

See Also box

picture caption

page number

article text

SET CONTENTS

CONTENTS BY CATEGORY

INSECTS

SPIDERS

OTHER ARTHROPODS

OVERVIEW

AFRICANIZED BEE

Often called killer bees, Africanized bees are an aggressive type of bee that are spreading across North and South America. They are descended from African honeybees that were imported to Brazil in the last century.

Bees are important for pollinating flowers, including those of fruit trees and many other crop plants. In 1956, a Brazilian bee expert named Warwick Kerr imported some African honeybees. He wanted to interbreed them with local bees to create a new strain of honeybee that would be better suited to the warm climate of Brazil. African honeybees are similar to other honeybees, but they are more aggressive and are more likely to sting people.

Unfortunately, a year after the experiments began, 26 colonies of the African honeybees were accidentally released into the wild. These bees started to breed with local wild types of honeybee, and a very aggressive hybrid strain of bee was produced. A hybrid is a cross between two different strains or species. By the 21st century, Africanized bees had spread across most of South and Central America and had reached as far north as Nevada.

▲ *Africanized bees at the entrance of an artificial hive. Scientists are studying the bees to find out how they can control the spread of these troublesome insects.*

KEY FACTS

Name
Africanized bee
(*Apis mellifera
scutellata*)

**Distinctive
features**
Almost identical
to European
honeybees but
much more
aggressive

Habitat
Warm wooded or
scrub areas

Food
Pollen and nectar

Size
Worker: 0.75
inches (19 mm)
long; queen: 1 inch
(25 mm) long

▼ *A swarm of
Africanized bees on
a tree. The colony
huddles in a mass
while scout bees
search for a suitable
nesting site.*

African honeybees and the African-ized hybrids look more or less identical to European strains of honeybees, although Africanized bees are a little smaller. European settlers brought honeybees to South America hundreds of years ago, and European strains have lived in the wild since then.

African bees are similar to the European forms in the way that they behave. However, the new Africanized bees differ from European strains in the way they feed, in their swarming behavior, and in their willingness to attack other animals in large numbers.

Pollen gatherers

Africanized honeybees seek out pollen and nectar from tropical plants, including plants with flowers that open during the night. The bees often live in places where water is in short supply, and they will move their nests several times in a year, looking for wetter areas. So, colonies of Africanized bees are less settled than European colonies.

European bees take food from a variety of plants and store a lot of their honey. Africanized bees do not store much honey, using it instead to feed their larvae and increase the number of bees in the colony. European strains eat their store of honey during the winter and are much better at surviving cold temperatures than the Africanized

DISTRIBUTION

☐ AFRICANIZED BEE

variety. Experts think that Africanized bees will not be able to spread much farther north or south into colder areas.

Swarming

Once the colony has grown large, many of the bees leave the nest in a swarm. Swarming generally happens during the spring and fall, when new colonies look for places to nest. Africanized bees are less choosy than European bees in picking nesting sites. While European bees prefer large spaces, Africanized bees often choose small parts of human constructions, such as sheds, attics, trash cans, and even old cars, as well as hollow trees and other natural crevices.

When Africanized bees are swarming, or when they are gathering pollen from flowers, they are unlikely to attack people. They are most aggressive when they have started raising young and if their nest is threatened.

On the attack

Colonies of Africanized bees are more sensitive to disturbance than those of European bees. They are often disturbed by everyday events, such as the vibrations from a passing vehicle,

power equipment, or just someone walking close to the nest. Once the colony is agitated, it can be dangerous to walk within a hundred yards of the nest. The bees have been known to chase people for nearly half a mile.

The venom of the Africanized bee is no worse than that of European honeybees. However, while European strains are slow to sting, Africanized bees sting readily and in great numbers. When agitated, a bee releases an alarm chemical that rouses the other bees. When a bee stings, it releases more of this substance, and other bees follow, attacking the unfortunate victim.

Killer bees

Africanized bees are sometimes called killer bees. However, they do not deserve this name. Most cases of people being stung to death are in areas where

▲ *A worker Africanized bee returns to the nest after foraging. The yellow lumps on the hind legs are baskets packed with pollen.*

SEE ALSO

- *Bee*
- *Bee fly*
- *Honeybee*
- *Pollination*
- *Social insect*
- *Wasp*

the victims have been unable to escape from the bees and medical treatment was not available quickly.

Five hundred bee stings are enough to kill a healthy adult human. However, some people are much more sensitive to the sting and one sting can cause them to go into shock and die.

Living with bees

Although Africanized bees are a pest, they have had little effect on colonies of other bee species that share their habitat. Despite efforts by people to control them, Africanized bees continue to extend their range. Even parasitic mites of the genus (group) *Varroa*, which have devastated colonies of other strains of honeybees, have little effect on Africanized bees. It seems people in North and South America will simply have to get used to them.

ALDERFLY

Alderflies spend most of their lives as larvae, preying on small invertebrates in ponds and lakes. The presence of alderfly larvae indicates that the water in which they live is not polluted.

Alderflies make up a small family of around 100 species. They are closely related to dobsonflies and are sometimes grouped with lacewings and ant lions as well. The adults are generally between 0.5 and 0.75 inches (13 and 19 mm) long and have soft brown or black bodies, with two pairs of wings.

The wings of alderflies are folded up, like a fan, where they attach to the insect's body. All four of an alderfly's wings are about the same size and have a smoky appearance, with dark wing veins. When at rest, the wings are held together like a tent over the back of the body. Unlike dobsonflies, adult alderflies tend to have a blunt, rather square head, with long, threadlike antennae and a single tail-like filament (threadlike structure) at the end of the abdomen. In addition, alderfly larvae have seven pairs of gill filaments, while dobsonflies have eight pairs.

The females lay a mat of up to 900 eggs in a single layer on rocks, plants, or other surfaces beside or overhanging water. The eggs are generally brown and are bullet shaped.

◀ *After emerging from its pupal chamber, an adult alderfly rests on a plant. Adults can often be seen beside ponds, lakes, and slow-moving rivers and streams.*

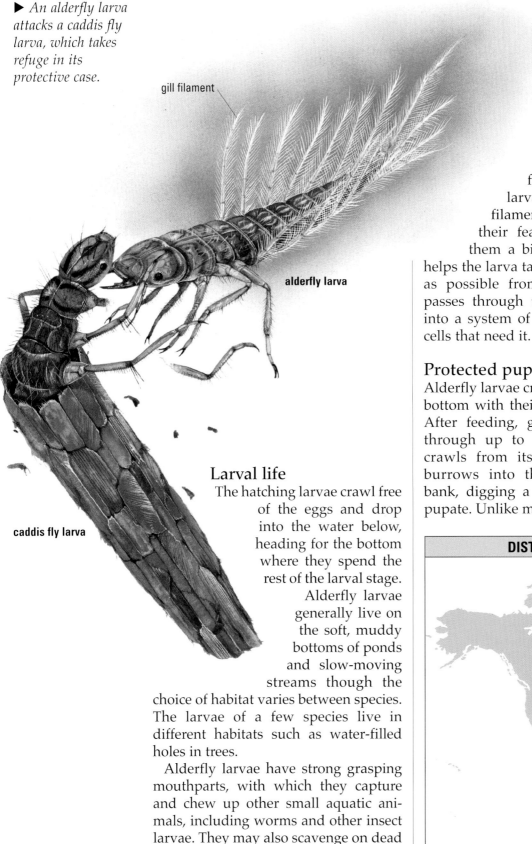

▶ *An alderfly larva attacks a caddis fly larva, which takes refuge in its protective case.*

gill filament

alderfly larva

caddis fly larva

Larval life

The hatching larvae crawl free of the eggs and drop into the water below, heading for the bottom where they spend the rest of the larval stage. Alderfly larvae generally live on the soft, muddy bottoms of ponds and slow-moving streams though the choice of habitat varies between species. The larvae of a few species live in different habitats such as water-filled holes in trees.

Alderfly larvae have strong grasping mouthparts, with which they capture and chew up other small aquatic animals, including worms and other insect larvae. They may also scavenge on dead animals that they chance upon. While the larvae are fierce underwater predators, adult alderflies do not feed at all.

Since alderfly larvae spend their lives beneath the surface of the water, these insects have unusual structures called gill filaments that extend from the body and allow the animal to take oxygen from the water. The larvae have seven pairs of filaments along the body, and their feathery structure gives them a big surface area, which helps the larva take up as much oxygen as possible from the water. Oxygen passes through the thin cuticle (skin) into a system of tubules, then into the cells that need it.

Protected pupae

Alderfly larvae crawl around the stream bottom with their well-developed legs. After feeding, growing, and molting through up to ten stages, the larva crawls from its watery habitat and burrows into the soil of the riverbank, digging a chamber in which to pupate. Unlike many pupae, an alderfly

DISTRIBUTION

▪ *SIALIS VELATA*
▪ *SIALIS BILOBATA*

▶ *A gill filament from a larval alderfly. Each larva has seven pairs of these filaments, and every filament has five segments. The filaments attach to plates on the side of the abdomen.*

pupa can move its legs and mouthparts, allowing it to deliver a sharp bite to predators even while its body is going through metamorphosis.

Emerging adults
When the pupa has completed its development, it wriggles up to the surface, and the adult insect emerges as it sheds its skin one last time. The adults do not live for very long, spending much of their brief lives seeking mates. When they are near one another, the males and females signal to each other by vibrating their abdomens, making a buzzing noise. The male transfers a gel-like package of sperm cells, called a spermatophore, to the female, and this fertilizes her eggs.

A long life cycle
The alderfly life cycle can take a long time to be completed. Most species take at least a year to complete their development, and some take even longer. The time each larva takes

to develop is strongly influenced by environmental conditions, such as the quality and amount of food available, and the temperature. As in most other species of insects, alderfly larvae develop more quickly when the temperature is higher.

Pollution indicators
Alderfly larvae are dependent on water that contains a lot of oxygen to survive. Pollution from houses and factories reduces the amount of oxygen available, causing alderfly numbers to drop. Because of this sensitivity, the number of alderfly larvae present is often used by scientists as an indicator of the health of a stretch of water.

Alderflies are common in North America. One of the most widespread is *Sialis velata*, which lives throughout eastern United States and Canada. New species are still being found; *Sialis bilobata*, from California, was discovered as recently as 1991.

▶ *An alderfly larva under water. These look similar to the larvae of lacewings, to which they are closely related.*

ANATOMY AND PHYSIOLOGY

Pumping blood, exchanging gases, digesting food, and passing out waste products are functions that are performed by organs in the bodies of insects and spiders.

Arthropods include insects, arachnids, and myriapods. They share several anatomical features, such as segmented bodies, hard exoskeletons, and jointed appendages. However, the ways in which these segments and appendages have become specialized to perform different functions are unique to each group. So, although insects and spiders may look somewhat similar, many features of their anatomy differ.

Segmentation

The bodies of all insects can be divided into three sections, which are composed of fused and specialized segments. The head contains the eyes, antennae, and mouthparts. The midbody, or thorax, has six legs attached, and where present, the wings. The final section, the abdomen, contains many organs, including the reproductive organs. In some groups, such as the wasps and ants, the abdomen is connected to the thorax via a narrow waist.

Spiders also have an abdomen, but the head and thorax of these animals are fused to form the cephalothorax, covered by a tough shield called the carapace. The legs of adult arthropods are jointed and powered by muscles, although spiders also use the pressure of their blood system.

The wings of insects are powered both by direct muscular movement and indirectly, by moving the walls of the thorax. Unlike the wings of vertebrates such as bats and birds, insect wings did not evolve from legs. Instead, they probably appeared as independent growths from the thorax that may have had a role in heat regulation before becoming useful for gliding, and ultimately for powered flight.

At the rear of the spider abdomen are the spinnerets, from which silk is extruded. Some spiders have a plate just in front of this, called the cribellum, which helps spin the silk.

Hearts and hemolymph

Humans have a closed circulatory system, with blood contained within arteries, veins, and capillaries. By contrast, insects have an open system, with the blood moving within the body

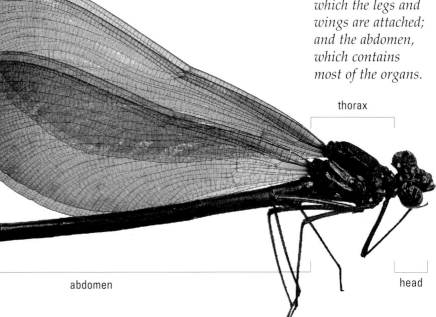

thorax

abdomen

head

▼ *The bodies of all insects, such as this dragonfly, can be divided into three main sections. These are the head, which contains the brain and many of the sensory organs as well as the feeding apparatus; the thorax, to which the legs and wings are attached; and the abdomen, which contains most of the organs.*

cavity (or hemocoel) and pouring from the ends of the arteries directly onto the tissues. However, both insects and humans use a heart that moves blood around the body. Unlike our heart, the insect heart is a long, tubular organ that is contained within the thorax and abdomen. Insects also have extra pumping organs, called pulsatile organs, at the bases of the wings and antennae, that help to keep the blood moving. Most insects move blood in a circulatory fashion, but some, such as beetles, simply shunt the blood between the thorax and the abdomen.

The blood itself, called hemolymph, bathes the tissues. It has a similar role to the blood of humans, transporting nutrients and waste products, as well as chemicals such as hormones, around the body. The hemolymph is yellow and contains cells called hemocytes that help to repair wounds and combat bacteria or larger internal parasites.

Taking in oxygen

Oxygen is an essential part of the metabolism of all animals. When combined with sugars and the right enzymes, a chemical reaction produces energy, which all organisms need to function. Waste products are also produced by this reaction in the form of water and carbon dioxide. Tiny arthropods, such as springtails, can simply exchange gases across the exoskeleton. Larger arthropods have more sophisticated systems. Some aquatic insects, such as larval blackflies, have gills. The gills of damselfly larvae are inside the rectum, and the insect must draw water into this cavity to take in oxygen. The amount of oxygen dissolved in the water is higher than that on the other side of the gill, and oxygen moves from

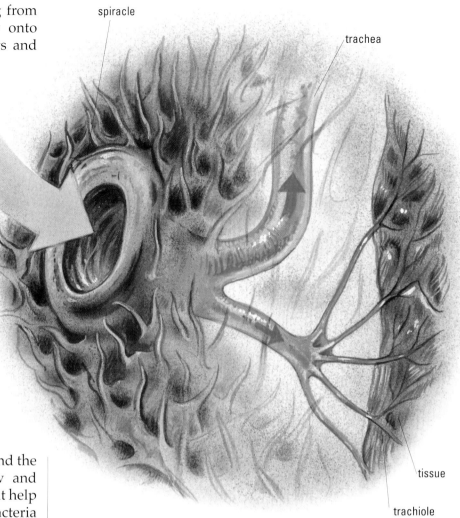

the region of high concentration to the region of low concentration. Carbon dioxide moves in the opposite direction, from the body into the water. The process by which gases such as these move is called diffusion.

Insects that live on land, and a few aquatic ones, use an alternative oxygen uptake strategy. They have a series of pores, called spiracles, through which air enters. The oxygen passes through a system of tubes, called tracheae, which are stiffened with circular rings of tissue that stop the tracheae from collapsing with changes in pressure. The tracheae end deep inside the body; there, the oxygen dissolves into a liquid and diffuses into the tissue, with carbon dioxide moving in the opposite direction. Larger insects ventilate the tracheae through a series of air sacs that

▲ *The tracheal system of an insect. Air enters through the spiracle. Unlike many other arthropods, insect spiracles can be closed by muscles, helping keep in moisture. Air passes into the tracheae, a series of tubes stiffened with tough rings. These branch into smaller trachioles, which end within the tissues. There, gaseous exchange takes place.*

▶ *Most spiders have book lungs. Gases move across the lamellae, between the hemolymph and the air.*

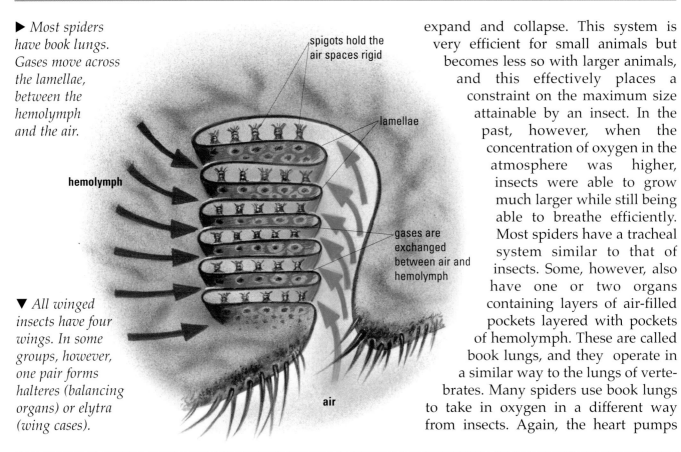

spigots hold the air spaces rigid

lamellae

hemolymph

gases are exchanged between air and hemolymph

air

▼ *All winged insects have four wings. In some groups, however, one pair forms halteres (balancing organs) or elytra (wing cases).*

expand and collapse. This system is very efficient for small animals but becomes less so with larger animals, and this effectively places a constraint on the maximum size attainable by an insect. In the past, however, when the concentration of oxygen in the atmosphere was higher, insects were able to grow much larger while still being able to breathe efficiently. Most spiders have a tracheal system similar to that of insects. Some, however, also have one or two organs containing layers of air-filled pockets layered with pockets of hemolymph. These are called book lungs, and they operate in a similar way to the lungs of vertebrates. Many spiders use book lungs to take in oxygen in a different way from insects. Again, the heart pumps

GENERAL ANATOMY OF AN INSECT

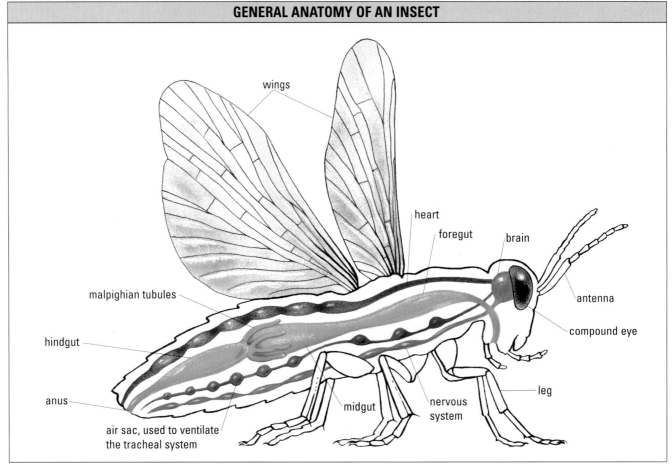

wings

heart

foregut

brain

antenna

compound eye

malpighian tubules

hindgut

anus

leg

midgut

nervous system

air sac, used to ventilate the tracheal system

hemolymph around the body, but a continuous flow through the book lungs is required. Spider hemolymph appears blue, due to a copper-containing pigment called hemocyanin. This pigment binds with oxygen in the book lung, from where it is carried to other tissues. Respiratory pigments such as this are rare in insects, but some insects that live in low-oxygen conditions, such as midge larvae in stagnant ponds, have a kind of hemoglobin similar to that found in human blood in their hemolymph.

Some aquatic insects and a few species of spiders have a structure called a plastron that holds a thin layer of air around the body, into which the spiracles open directly.

Digestion and absorption

After passing through the mouthparts, food enters the foregut; this is mainly used for storage, but insects that eat solid food, such as grasshoppers and beetles, also have grinding plates here that break up food. The food then moves to the midgut, where it is digested. Specialized cells secrete a coating called a peritrophic envelope that covers the food. The peritrophic envelope keeps harmful chemicals at bay, including tannin, which is

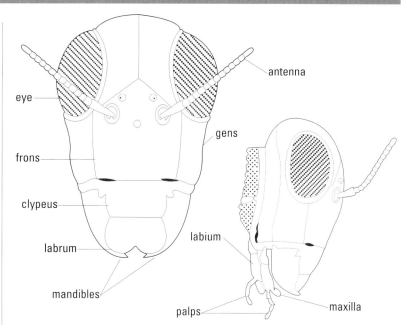

commonly found in leaves, as well as bacteria. It may also help the flow of digestive juices through the food. Other cells in the wall of the midgut secrete enzymes—these are proteins that help digest food, breaking it down into easily absorbable sugars and fats. The walls of the midgut are folded into tiny bumps called microvilli; these increase the surface area available for the absorption of nutrients.

Tiny microbes live in the midguts of some insects, such as termites. These break down compounds such as plant cellulose into an easily digestible form.

▲ *The head and mouthparts of a typical insect. The labrum and mandibles are often used for cropping vegetation or for biting prey. The palps are used to taste food and push it into the mouth. However, many insects have highly modified mouthparts that differ greatly from this generalized body plan.*

Reproduction in insects and spiders

Sexual reproduction, where the eggs of a female are fertilized by sperm from a male, is common in insects, although some reproduce asexually and do not require sperm. When the sexes come together, one commonly mounts the back of the other. The male often grasps the female, using the legs or modified wings. Male dragonflies have claspers on the end of the abdomen with which to hold the female. Most male insects have an organ called an aedeagus with which sperm is introduced into a genital chamber within the body of the female. The sperm may be packaged into a bundle called spermatophore. Sperm is stored in the female in a vessel called a spermatheca—in some insects, such as the queens of social insects, the sperm can remain there for years.

Eggs are produced inside the ovaries of the female. They are fertilized by sperm from the spermatheca as they pass into the genital chamber. Fertilization fuses sperm and egg, producing an embryo with genetic material from both the male and the female. The eggs pass along tubes to the ovipositor, or egg tube, which usually opens at the tip of the abdomen. As they pass glands, the eggs may be coated with substances that help them stick. The eggs are laid on a suitable surface via the ovipositor, although some insects hatch while still inside the female. The internal anatomy of spiders is similar, but there is one major difference. Instead of an aedeagus, males introduce sperm into the female using the palps, leglike appendages near the mouth. The end of the palp of some species break off within the female genital duct (or epigyne), stopping the palps of other males from entering and fertilizing the eggs.

GENERAL ANATOMY OF A SPIDER

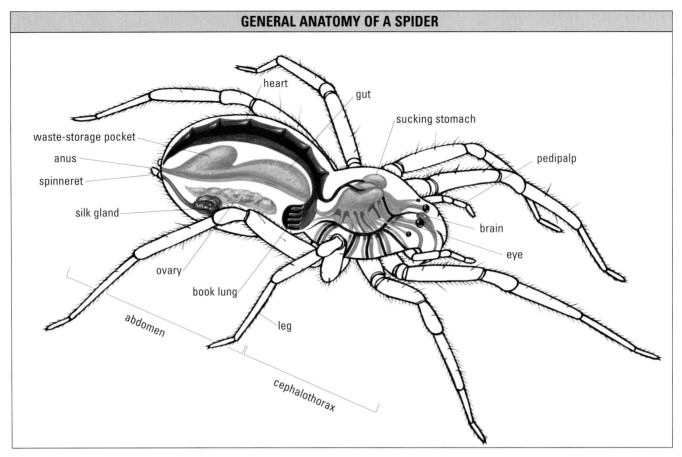

heart

gut

sucking stomach

waste-storage pocket

anus

spinneret

silk gland

pedipalp

brain

eye

ovary

book lung

abdomen

leg

cephalothorax

▲ *The anatomy of a spider. Spiders have four pairs of legs and a body that is divided into two parts.*

Water is absorbed from the food through a series of pads in the rectum, which is part of the hindgut. Many aquatic insects have specialized cells in the hindgut called chloride cells. These cells draw particles from water as it is drawn into the rectum. The waste products of metabolism are often toxic and must either be converted and stored in a nontoxic form (usually as a chemical called uric acid) or be removed swiftly. Both insects and spiders achieve this using a system of tubes called the malpighian tubules. These remove waste from the hemolymph, producing

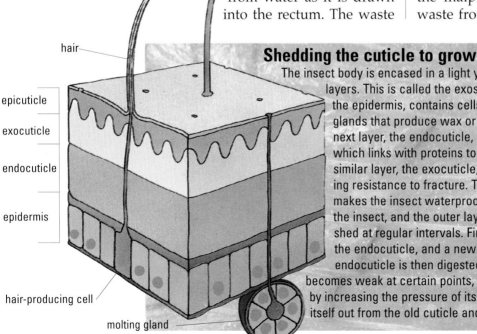

hair

epicuticle

exocuticle

endocuticle

epidermis

hair-producing cell

molting gland

Shedding the cuticle to grow

The insect body is encased in a light yet tough skin, divided into several layers. This is called the exoskeleton, or cuticle. The inner layer, the epidermis, contains cells that produce hairs, as well as glands that produce wax or enzymes that trigger molting. The next layer, the endocuticle, is rich in a compound called chitin, which links with proteins to give structure to the cuticle. A similar layer, the exocuticle, is sclerotized (hardened), providing resistance to fracture. The outermost layer, the epicuticle, makes the insect waterproof. The cuticle does not grow with the insect, and the outer layers of the exoskeleton must be shed at regular intervals. First, the epidermis separates from the endocuticle, and a new cuticle begins to form. The endocuticle is then digested by molting enzymes. The cuticle becomes weak at certain points, and the insect splits the old cuticle by increasing the pressure of its hemolymph. The insect then draws itself out from the old cuticle and waits for the new one to harden.

liquid urine. The urine passes to the hindgut, where much of the water and some salts are reabsorbed, leaving a concentrated paste to be voided from the anus. This process allows land-living insects and spiders to conserve valuable water. In aquatic insects and those that feed on sap, such as aphids, there is little need for such water conservation, and the urine is more liquid. Some insects, such as lacewings, use the malpighian tubules for silk production, and some flies use the secretions to toughen up the walls of their pupae.

Spiders never swallow solid food but use their sucking stomach to ingest the liquefied tissues of their prey. From the stomach, the liquid passes into the many branches of the midgut, where food is further broken down and the nutrients are absorbed. The end of the midgut widens into a chamber. This connects to the anus via a short hindgut.

The importance of glands
Many aspects of an arthropod's life are controlled by hormones. These are chemicals that circulate through the hemolymph of the animal and control long-term physiological and behavioral

SEE ALSO
- *Ant*
- *Arthropod*
- *Beetle*
- *Bug*
- *Defense*
- *Dragonfly and damselfly*
- *Feeding*
- *Fly*
- *Insect life cycle*
- *Larva, nymph, and pupa*
- *Locomotion*
- *Metamorphosis*
- *Moth and butterfly*
- *Senses*
- *Spider*

▼ *Young insects, such as this caterpillar, do not have adult structures such as wings. Adult features develop during metamorphosis from a series of buds.*

characteristics. For example, the change from larva to pupa is controlled by hormones, as is the absorption of water in the rectum. Glands are specialized tissues that produce and secrete hormones, along with a range of other important substances. Glands provide gel-like coatings for eggs, secrete pheromones, and produce copious amounts of saliva for insects that digest their food outside the body, like blowflies, and also for spiders. Glands are responsible for producing the defensive chemicals of many insects, including the toxic cocktail that bombardier beetles squirt at predators.

Spiders also have a range of specialized glands. They have many silk glands in the abdomen, each kind producing a different type of silk. These glands lead via a short duct to the spinnerets. The silk is teased out using specialized claws on the rear legs. Most glands do not have muscles to squeeze out their secretions; exceptions include the poison glands of spiders. A powerful pump injects venom into their victims because spiders need to subdue struggling prey as quickly as possible.

ANT

Ants are very successful insects that live in almost all land habitats on Earth. One reason for ants' success is their efficient social organization.

In many ways, ants are typical insects. Their body is composed of three distinct parts: a head, a thorax, and an abdomen. They have six jointed legs attached to the thorax (midbody), a pair of jawlike mandibles, and two bent antennae attached to the head.

Unlike many insects, however, most ants do not have wings. Although they have large compound eyes, ants use their senses of smell and taste much more than their vision. All ants have a tiny segment that joins the thorax to the abdomen. This narrow waist is called a petiole.

Waspish relations

It is easy to mistake some wasps for ants, because they also have a petiole. Indeed, ants are very closely related to wasps, and scientists think that the two groups had a common ancestor during the Cretaceous period, more than 130 million years ago. Today, ants and wasps are grouped together, along with bees and sawflies, in an insect order called the Hymenoptera. Although termites look like ants and have similar habits, they are not closely related to them. Around 9,000 species of ants have been discovered and described by

▼ *A cross section of a worker ant. The glands are used for communication between ants. Dufour's gland releases alarm pheromones, as do the mandibular and pygidial glands. Pavan's gland releases feeding trail pheromones to show other ants where to find food.*

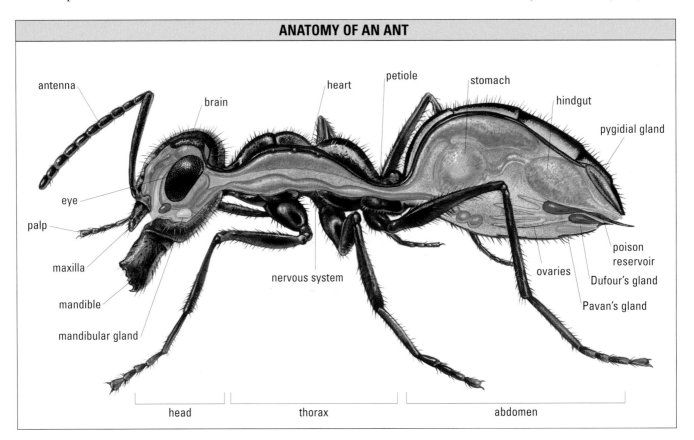

ANATOMY OF AN ANT

antenna
brain
heart
petiole
stomach
hindgut
pygidial gland
eye
palp
maxilla
mandible
mandibular gland
nervous system
ovaries
poison reservoir
Dufour's gland
Pavan's gland

head
thorax
abdomen

DISTRIBUTION

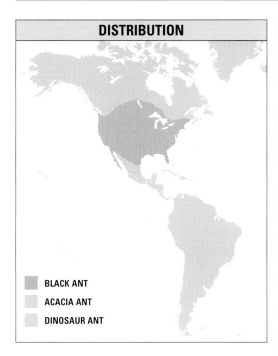

- BLACK ANT
- ACACIA ANT
- DINOSAUR ANT

scientists so far, and new ones are being found all the time. Most ants live in the hot tropics, but these insects also make their home in grasslands and forests all over the world. The only place ants have yet to be found is in the cold, icy regions around the poles.

Society queens
Ants are very sociable and live together in highly organized groups, or colonies. Scientists describe them as social insects because different ants have different roles within the colony; they cooperate in caring for the young and help rear several generations in their lifetime. Unlike their cousins bees and wasps, which have just a few social species each, all ants share this behavior.

Some ant societies are huge, while others are very small. For example, colonies of east African driver ants contain up to 22 million individuals, while those of the Brazilian dinosaur ant have an average of just 13 ants.

Within an ant society, all the ants work together to keep the colony running like clockwork. Most ants in a colony are sisters that have hatched from eggs laid by one mother, called the queen. The queen ant is the only ant in a colony that can reproduce. Whether one of the queen's daughters develops into another queen depends on several things. The queens of some species of ants suppress the production of other queens by releasing pheromones (chemical messages). In other species, the amount of food available, the temperature inside the nest, egg size, or the age of the queen determines the ants' development. Male ants are generally produced once a year.

Workers unite
Nearly all the ants in a colony are female worker ants. They are called workers because they perform all the tasks inside and outside the nest, such as foraging for food, defending the colony against attacks from other animals, repairing and cleaning the nest, and taking care of the queen and her offspring. The workers of some species try to lay their own eggs, but the queen or other workers usually eat them.

All the workers of most ant species look exactly the same. However, the workers of some species are divided into different types depending on the job they do. This is particularly obvious in the tropical leaf-cutting ants, which collect leaves on which to grow fungus in underground gardens. Leaf-cutting soldiers are 300 times larger than the

▼ *An army ant queen with a worker. The queen's abdomen is swollen to a huge size by the eggs inside.*

When organisms reproduce, they pass genetic material, or genes, to their offspring. Genes form the code that controls the development of any living organism. Although worker ants do not reproduce, they still ensure their genes reach the next generation. Each worker carries genetic material inherited from its parents: half from the queen and half from a male. On average, the workers share three-quarters of their genes with other workers, so they are more closely related to their sisters than their parents. By nurturing the queen, worker ants make sure more of their genes are likely to be passed on, and in greater numbers, than if they reproduced themselves. If workers controlled the development of larvae, they would make more queens so more of their genes could be passed on. The queen needs workers, however, and prevents the development of new queens with pheromones.

▲ *These ants are carrying a wasp back to the nest. Although they often feed on the dead, many ants will prey on any small animal that is too slow to escape.*

tiniest workers. Many species of ants have soldiers with large mouthparts for defending the colony from attack, and some squirt chemicals at enemies.

Some ants have no workers of their own. Instead, they make slaves of other species of ants. These parasitic ants enter and take over the hosts' nest. They

▶ *Winged black ants before their nuptial (mating) flight. The larger ants are females. Winged ants from many colonies emerge at the same time, so they have a better chance of finding a mate. This is why the skies fill with winged ants on just a couple of days each year.*

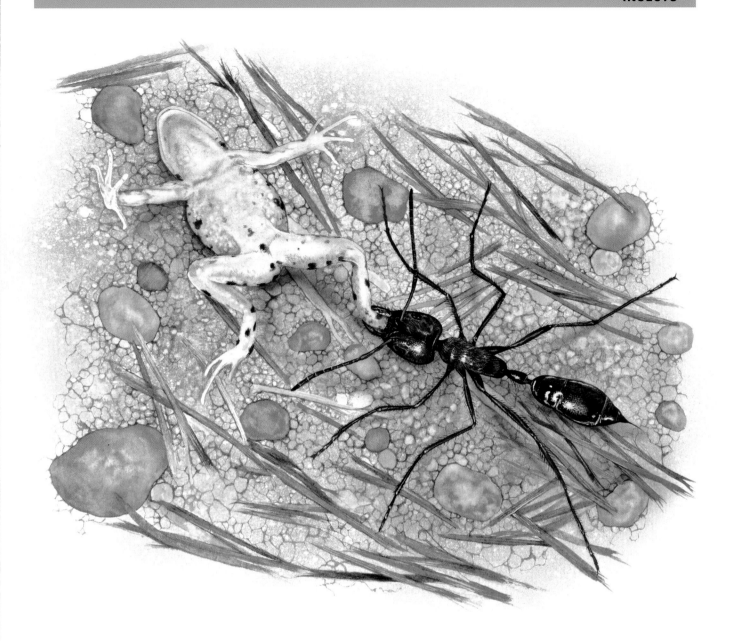

kill the resident queen and steal the eggs and younger larvae. The slave-making ants then raise the young to be their slaves in their colony.

Nuptial flights

All worker ants are wingless insects, but every year most ant colonies produce winged males and queens. The job of these ants is to fly out from the nest and mate with ants from other colonies, after which the newly mated queens set up nests of their own. Every colony in a neighborhood sends out its winged ants at exactly the same time, which is why the sidewalk is covered in flying ants on

just one or two days of the year. Mating with queens from other colonies is the only task that male ants have to perform, and they die soon after the nuptial flights. Each queen stores sperm inside her body. She loses her wings and digs a small chamber in the soil into which she lays her eggs. While the workers grow, the queen is kept alive by her stored fat and by breaking down her unneeded wing muscles.

Budding colonies

Not all ant colonies reproduce by sending out flying ants, however. For example, little fire ant colonies simply

▲ *Dinosaur ants are among the largest ants in the world. They prey mainly on insects but will also feed on dead animals. This ant is dragging a small frog back to the nest.*

▶ *These black ants are communicating through touch. They are guarding a group of aphids from predators. The ants feed on honeydew, a sweet-tasting liquid that the aphids secrete from their abdomens.*

KEY FACTS

Name
Black ant
(*Lasius niger*)

Distinctive features
Small black ant living in large colonies in and around homes

Habitat
Suburban gardens, under sidewalks, and in buildings; also lives in forests

Behavior
Lives in large complex societies in underground nest; protects aphids, feeding on honeydew in return

Breeding
Queen produces winged reproductive ants once each year

Food
Nectar, insects, fruit, honeydew

Size
Workers: 0.2 inches (5 mm) long

expand outward. New queens each take a small group of workers and set up home a short distance from their mother's nest. Making a new colony in this way is called budding.

Nesting instinct

Most ants' colonies make their home in nests that they build or dig themselves. Many of these are located underground, and some are huge. For example, the nest of a leaf-cutting ant colony may be as large as a human house and consist of hundreds of chambers.

Some ants, such as the red imported fire ant, top their nests with mounds of soil or vegetation. This helps keep the nest warm below, and the ants move the queen and larvae to different levels of the mound to find the most suitable temperature. Other ants live in rotten logs or holes in tree trunks, and there are even some species that live only in the hollow thorns of acacia trees.

One thing all ants' nests have in common is that they are dark inside. As a result, ants rely heavily on touch and the release of chemicals to communicate with each other. These insects use a whole range of different chemical signals to recognize each other and to give each other information about the colony, enemies that are nearby, and where food can be found.

Ant–plant relationships

Plants are under constant attack from herbivorous (plant-eating) insects and other animals. Some species hire the help of ants for protection. Many plants have sources of nectar that are not involved in pollination. Instead, the nectar attracts ants, which feed on it and also forage for herbivorous insects on the plant.

Acacia trees provide not only food for ants but lodgings as well. The ants nest within hollow thorns on the tree. In return, the ants protect the plant from both insect herbivores and larger mammals. These ants are so fierce that army ants avoid acacia trees for fear of tangling with their ant guards.

Often the relationship between ant and plant is extremely close. *Leonardoxa* plants are guarded by ants that feed on nectar from the plants' flowers. The plant signals to the ants using chemicals, leading them to new shoots and leaves. The ants then concentrate their defensive efforts on these vulnerable parts of the plant.

Some ants, such as army ants, do not have permanent nests at all, because they are constantly on the move. Instead, they make temporary nests (called bivouacs) at night, using their own bodies to shelter the queen and her developing offspring.

Life and death

Ants feed on a wide variety of different foods. Some species are carnivorous and hunt down other insects, spiders, scorpions, and sometimes the young of larger animals. Others are herbivorous, feeding on nectar from flowers, leaves, or other vegetation.

There are even ants that practice agriculture or livestock farming, feeding on fungi they have grown, seeds they have harvested, or a sweet sugary liquid called honeydew. This they get as payment for protecting certain species of bugs and caterpillars. In most species, when an ant finds a particularly good food source, she leaves a trail of pheromones along the ground as she returns home. This allows her nestmates to follow the trail, find the food, and help bring it back to the nest.

▼ *Inside a red ant nest. The white grubs are pupae—the stage between larvae and adults.*

The main enemies of ants are other ants. Many species defend themselves by biting with their slicing mandibles and stinging with the tip of the abdomen. Most animals go out of the way to avoid ants. The bite or sting is often painful, and they can attack in great numbers. Nonetheless, there are several ant-eating spider, mammal, and reptile species.

Important insects

Even though they are small, ants have been very common land animals for millions of years and are often essential members of the habitats in which they live. Many ants are regarded as pests by humans because they strip leaves off plants, cause damage to homes, and get into supplies of food.

Most of the biggest pest species today, such as the fire ants (so called because they can give a burning sting), have been introduced by people to areas of the world where they have no natural predators. However, many ant species are beneficial, since they keep numbers of pest insects down. Their digging also enriches soil as it mixes nutrients.

ANT-DECAPITATING FLY

Dead ants without heads can sometimes be found within a trail of ants. These unfortunate workers have been beheaded by the maggot of a tiny parasite, the ant-decapitating fly.

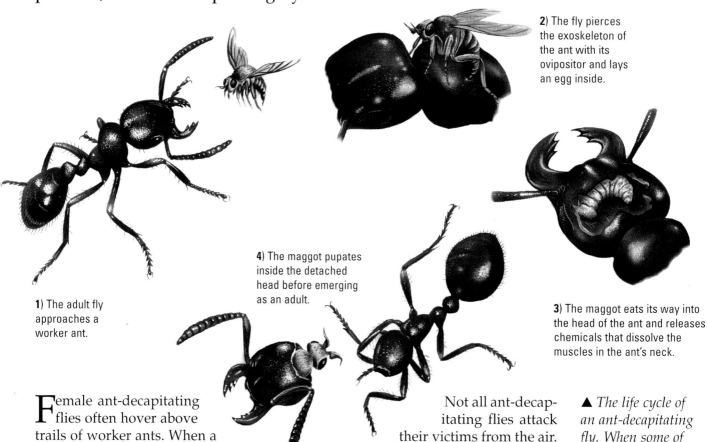

2) The fly pierces the exoskeleton of the ant with its ovipositor and lays an egg inside.

4) The maggot pupates inside the detached head before emerging as an adult.

1) The adult fly approaches a worker ant.

3) The maggot eats its way into the head of the ant and releases chemicals that dissolve the muscles in the ant's neck.

Female ant-decapitating flies often hover above trails of worker ants. When a female has chosen a worker, she darts down and lands on the ant. The female then thrusts her sharp, swordlike ovipositor (egg tube) into the ant and lays a single egg. The victim is stunned but soon returns to its work.

After about ten days, however, the egg inside hatches into a hungry maggot that feeds on the internal organs of the ant. It eventually wriggles into the head, where it eats the contents. Before the maggot pupates, it produces enzymes that dissolve the tissues connecting the ant's head and thorax. This causes the head to drop off. The severed head is a safe, sheltered place inside which the pupa can develop.

Not all ant-decapitating flies attack their victims from the air. Females of an ant-decapitating fly from Texas run up to leaf-cutting ants and thrust their ovipositors between the ants' mouthparts. The ants defend themselves by retreating into the nest.

Entomologists estimate that there are more than 400 species of ant-decapitating flies worldwide, but only a few have been given names. Because these flies kill many ants and interrupt their foraging, scientists are beginning to use ant-decapitating flies to control the spread of pest ants. Ant-decapitating flies have been brought from Brazil to the southern United States to help control fire ants, which cannot find food efficiently in the presence of these little flies.

▲ *The life cycle of an ant-decapitating fly. When some of a colony's ants have been attacked by flies, all the workers are less likely to leave the nest, even the maggot-free ants.*

SEE ALSO

- *Ant*
- *Biological control*
- *Fire ant*
- *Leaf-cutting ant*
- *Parasitic fly*

ANT LION

Adult ant lions are rarely seen, but the conical pits made by their larvae are familiar sights in sand or dry soils. Small insects tumble into the pits and are devoured by the ant lions.

Ant lions are well-known insects, mostly due to the pitfall traps constructed by their strange-looking larvae. These pits are generally around 1 inch (2.5 cm) across, with sloping sides, and are dug into dry sand.

The adults are rarely seen because they are nocturnal (night active) insects. They look like damselflies, although their wings are usually partly wrapped around their long, soft body.

Building a trap

The larvae are sometimes called doodlebugs. They build their traps by digging a cone-shaped pit in the sand. The larva does this by shuffling in a circle, flicking sand over the rim with its head. This leaves a pillar in the center of the pit, which the doodlebug demolishes and clears before finally burying itself in the sand, where it waits for prey to drop in.

Ants and other small insects that stumble into one of these pits have trouble clambering back to the top because the sand is very loose. The doodlebug makes it even harder by flicking sand at its prey with its head.

Sucking out the internal organs

The jawlike mandibles of doodlebugs are deeply grooved on their undersides. Each groove is closed off by another section of the mouthparts called the

KEY FACTS

Name
Ant lions (Family Myrmeleontidae)

Distinctive features
Adults similar to damselflies but with clubbed antennae; larvae have fat bodies and long, sickle-shaped mandibles

Habitat
Open sandy soils

Food
Trap and eat ants and other small insects

Lifespan
Some larvae take up to 3 years to develop

▶ *An adult ant lion. These insects have narrow wing roots. This reduces air resistance, making flying less of an effort, but prevents ant lions from flying quickly.*

29

▲ *This ant lion larva has been exposed from its pit but will quickly dig a new one. The enormous jaws, or mandibles, are fringed with barbs that pierce the body of its insect prey.*

Pupating in the pit

In spring or early summer, the larva pupates in a ball-shaped cocoon at the bottom of the pit. After pupation, the delicate, night-flying adult emerges from the cocoon. At most, adults live for a few summer weeks before scattering their eggs on the sand and dying soon after. The larvae hatch and burrow into the sand for the winter and re-surface in spring to build their pits and await prey. Ant lions can spend up to three years as larvae.

Ant lion enemies

Pit-making ant lions live throughout the warmer parts of the world. The ant lion most often found on North American beaches is known simply as the common ant lion. This species is particularly widespread along the shores of the Great Lakes. There, the doodlebugs are often attacked by the larvae of a parasitic bee fly that lives only around the Great Lakes.

These ant lions are also attacked by wasps that let themselves be grasped between the long mandibles of the doodlebug. This dangerous strategy allows the wasp to place an egg between

maxillae. This arrangement makes a hollow structure not unlike a hypodermic syringe. After capturing its prey, the doodlebug injects a fast-acting venom through its mouthparts, before sucking out the internal organs.

Some ant lions do not make pits but hide under plant material or soil before ambushing their prey. One group, called the butterfly lions, cover just their bodies, leaving the heads visible.

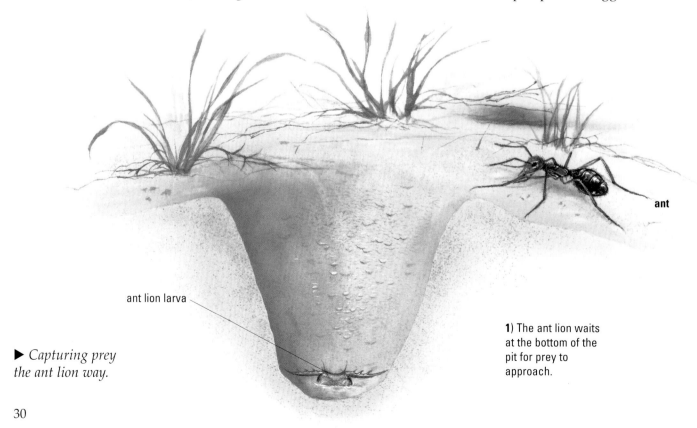

▶ *Capturing prey the ant lion way.*

ant lion larva

ant

1) The ant lion waits at the bottom of the pit for prey to approach.

the doodlebug's jaws. The wasp egg hatches into an internal parasite that eats the doodlebug from the inside out.

Ant lions belong to the insect order Neuroptera. Other neuropterans, such as lacewings, sponge flies, and owl flies, also have larvae with hollow mandibles for sucking out prey's body contents. These insects are sometimes grouped with the alderflies and dobsonflies, although the larvae of these insects chew their food. Like other neuropterans, adult ant lions feed on nectar and sweet liquids, and sometimes insects.

Worm lions

Pits remarkably similar to those made by ant lions are made by vermilionid fly larvae, which are also called worm lions. Worm lion pits look just like those of ant lions, and the larvae even flick sand at prey in a similar fashion. Worm lions are maggots that do not look anything like the broad, six-legged ant lion larvae. They are also much rarer than ant lions, with only a couple of species known to live in North America, in contrast to the hundred or so North American ant lion species.

▲ *An adult ant lion at rest. These insects occasionally feed on small insects but generally drink nectar from flowers.*

SEE ALSO
• *Alderfly*
• *Bee fly*
• *Dobsonfly*
• *Feeding*
• *Lacewing*
• *Larva, nymph, and pupa*
• *Sponge fly*

3) With the ant captured, the ant lion larva injects fast-acting poison. It then sucks out the internal organs of the ant through its mandibles.

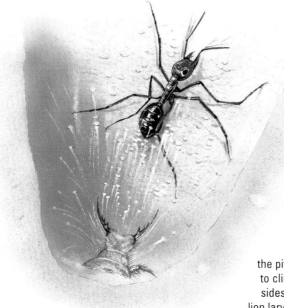

2) An ant tumbles into the pit. It is unable to climb the steep sides, and the ant lion larva flicks sand to knock it down.

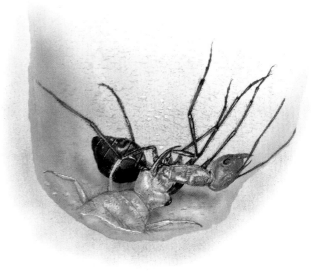

APHID

Aphids are bugs that feed by sucking the sap from plants. They can reproduce without mating, allowing very rapid population booms, and can be serious pests to many crops.

Aphids are pear-shaped bugs, belonging to the same large group of insects as cicadas and pond skaters. They are mostly small, ranging from between 0.04 and 0.2 inches (1 and 5 mm) long. Also called plant lice, these insects are common in gardens, greenhouses, and cultivated fields, where they can be very serious pests.

Like other bugs, such as assassin bugs, stinkbugs, and treehoppers, aphids have slender piercing and sucking mouthparts with interlocking parts that form a hollow tube. The insects use this tube to suck juices from the leaves and stems of plants. Their waste leaves the body in the form of honeydew, a sweet, sticky fluid that is nutritious to other insects such as ants.

Most aphids have a well-developed pair of cornicles—tubelike structures on the fifth or sixth segment of the abdomen. These secrete defensive chemicals that repel attackers. Many species can also produce protective waxes. Aphids do not always have wings. Winged aphids hold their wings over the body like a roof.

Life cycle and reproduction

During the summer, aphids may move from woody shrubs to smaller plants that live for only one season. Before winter begins, many of the migrant aphids return to the longer-lived woody plants before the colder weather kills off their summer host.

The aphid life cycle is very complicated. Aphids spend the winter as fertilized eggs laid on or near their primary food plants. All of the aphids that hatch in the spring are wingless females that are able to give birth to young without needing a mate—this process is called parthenogenesis. The next generation is born alive—the eggs hatch while still inside their mother. Some of these nymphs grow into winged females that fly off to other plants and settle down to feed and give birth to another generation of wingless females. This and future generations continue to produce more and more offspring by

◀ *A rose aphid on a thorn. Almost all land plants are fed upon by at least one species of aphid.*

parthenogenesis throughout the summer, enabling the aphid population to build up its numbers quickly. When a plant becomes overcrowded, winged females are produced, which fly off to plants that are uninhabited by aphids.

In the fall, the aphids give birth to males and females. Often, these have wings, so they can fly to woody plants that will survive the winter. The two sexes mate with each other, and the female lays fertilized eggs, which then lie dormant until spring.

Nearly every kind of land plant is fed upon by at least one type of aphid. Aphids can cause damage to the plants by disrupting the development of flowers and fruit and by spreading plant diseases. They may cause the plants to produce swellings called galls.

Enemies and defense

Aphids are an important source of food for many animals. Many types of insects, including ladybugs, larval hover flies, and larval green and brown lacewings, regularly attack and eat aphids. Aphids can also catch a variety of diseases. Fungal infections are common, and scientists have used fungi to help control pest species.

Many aphid species are parasitized by various wasps and flies. Parasites live on or inside a host animal on which they feed. One group of parasitic wasps specializes on aphids. The narrow waist of the female wasp allows the parasite to bend her abdomen under her body and thrust it forward to lay a single egg inside the body of an aphid. The wasp larva grows quickly, eating its host's insides, causing the aphid's body to swell and darken. Once an adult, the wasp chews a hole through the dead body of the aphid. The skins of dead aphids, or mummies, can often be seen among groups of living aphids.

Many species of aphids produce an alarm pheromone, a chemical that warns the group of danger. In the

▲ *This wingless adult aphid is surrounded by younger nymphs. Reproduction by parthenogenesis does not produce great variation; all the insects on this plant are genetically identical.*

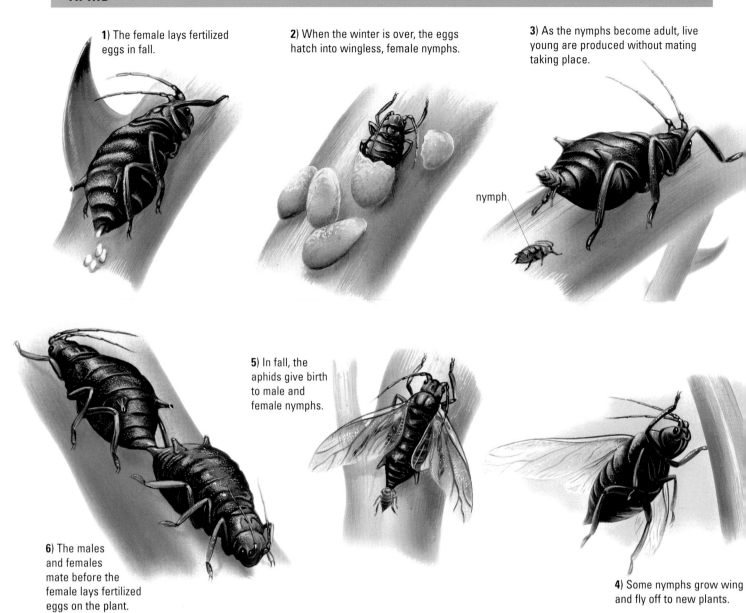

1) The female lays fertilized eggs in fall.

2) When the winter is over, the eggs hatch into wingless, female nymphs.

3) As the nymphs become adult, live young are produced without mating taking place.

nymph

5) In fall, the aphids give birth to male and female nymphs.

6) The males and females mate before the female lays fertilized eggs on the plant.

4) Some nymphs grow wing and fly off to new plants.

▲ *The life cycle of a black bean aphid. The sexual stages of this species are either wingless or winged. If the host plant is crowded with aphids, winged females will be born, which fly away to breed elsewhere. If the population is low, then the breeding aphids are usually wingless.*

presence of this pheromone, all the aphids in the group will engage in defensive tactics against a predator. They may kick out with their legs or fall from the plant to escape.

Some aphids use different methods to warn other aphids nearby. They stomp their feet or tap their abdomens on the stem of the plant. The signal vibrates through the stem and is transmitted to other aphids nearby.

Defense with soldiers

Some species of aphids have a sterile caste (type) of aphid called soldiers. These tiny defenders attack predators and their eggs with their long mouth-parts. One bamboo-eating species has soldiers that use the sharp horns on their heads and powerful grasping forelegs to attack hover fly larvae.

Aphids that feed on toxic plants, such as oleander and milkweed, are often bright yellow. These bright colors warn potential predators that the aphids are as poisonous and taste just as bad as the plants on which they feed.

Honeydew and ants

The waste product of aphids is called honeydew. It is a sweet liquid that contains a lot of sugar, and other insects find it very tasty. Some aphids release honeydew by flicking their abdomens to

Aphidlike bugs

Two families of bugs are closely related to true aphids. These include the woolly conifer aphids, which feed on the needles of conifers and sometimes cause swellings called galls. These bugs differ from aphids in that they lack cornicles. Also, they do not give birth to live young but lay eggs, though this can take place without fertilization. These insects feed on different plants at different times. The primary host is a spruce, but the bugs also feed on other conifers.

Phylloxeran bugs also lack cornicles, and unlike aphids, they hold their wings flat over the body. Some species can be serious pests; the introduced vine phylloxeran almost wiped out the North American wine industry in the nineteenth century.

shake off the drops. The sticky blobs attract butterflies, flies, bees, and ants. Some ants milk aphids, making them produce honeydew by stroking the aphids with their antennae. In return for this tasty food, the ants care for the aphids by driving off predators and parasitic animals. Some ants move aphids into shelters constructed from soil and leaves.

Among the best known of these aphid-milking ants are the black *Lasius* ants. These ants care for aphid eggs in their own nest in the winter, placing the young aphids on plants in spring. The dairy ant carefully places aphid nymphs on the roots of corn.

The relationship between ants and aphids is an example of a mutualism, a relationship in which both parties benefit from each other's presence. The ants receive food, while the aphids are given protection. The larvae of aphid-eating green lacewings avoid ant attacks by disguising themselves as aphids. The

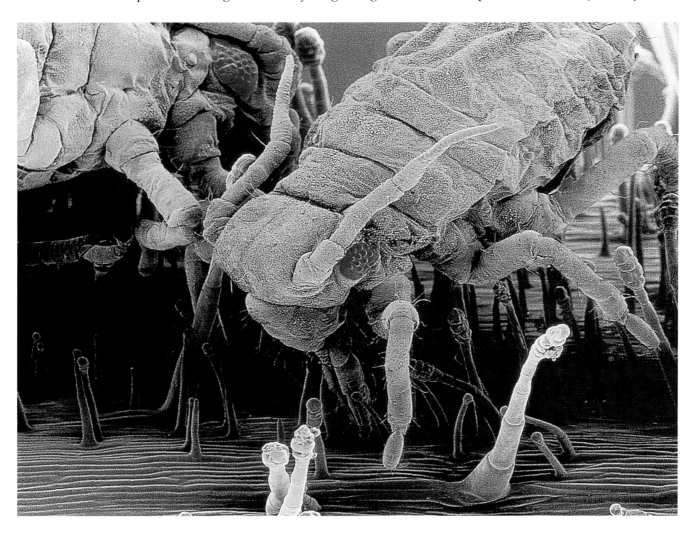

▼ *A scanning electron microscope has been used to generate this false-color image of aphids feeding on a leaf. The mouth-parts can be seen tapping into the sap of the plant, as can the individual lenses of the compound eyes.*

KEY WORDS

Cornicle
Bump on the abdomen that releases alarm pheromones

Gall
Swelling on a leaf formed by the plant's defense system

Honeydew
Sugary food waste secreted by aphids

Parthenogenesis
Reproduction without mating

green lacewing larva plucks the cottony wax coatings from its dead victims and attaches them to its own body, effectively disguising itself as a giant aphid. This disguise allows the larva to consume its prey without being attacked by the ants that guard the aphids. It is probable that rather than looking like an aphid, the lacewing larva fools the ants because of the aphids' chemical secretions contained within the wax.

Aphids and humans

Although aphids can damage plants by their feeding activities alone, it is their ability to transmit plant diseases that makes them important plant pests. They spread the organisms that cause plant diseases, such as the mosaic viruses, which affect plants such as sugar cane, tobacco, and cauliflower. Other diseases spread by aphids include parsnip yellow fleck, carrot redleaf, and cabbage black ring spot. Some viruses are spread directly from the aphid mouthparts, while others are drawn into the stomach of the insect. There, they multiply before being passed to another plant.

The honeydew produced by aphids can also cause problems. A small splash of honeydew acts as an ideal place for fungi to grow on plants. Leaves can become blackened with sooty mold, which cuts off light. Plants need light in order to produce the sugars that sustain them. Mold may also accumulate as an unsightly residue on cars, driveways, and sidewalks located beneath plants that are infested with aphids.

▶ *After landing on a suitable plant, this winged aphid gives birth to flightless nymphs. This takes place without the aphid mating, in a process called parthenogenesis. This process allows the population of aphids on the plant to build up very quickly.*

SEE ALSO

- *Biological control*
- *Bug*
- *Insect life cycle*
- *Leaf bug*
- *Mealybug*
- *Pest*
- *Scale*
- *Symbiosis*
- *Whitefly*

ARACHNOLOGY

Arachnology is the study of arachnids to help cure disease, make new materials, or learn more about this large group of animals, which includes spiders, mites, and scorpions.

KEY WORDS

Arachnid
Land-living animal with eight legs

Harvestman
Spiderlike animal with long legs and one body segment

Tick and mite
Tiny arachnids; many suck blood

Scorpion
Well-armed arachnids with pincers and a stinger

Spider
Two body segments; most spiders have venomous fangs

Sun spider
Spiderlike animal with massive mouthparts

Whip scorpion
Scorpion-like animal with whip-tail but no stinger

Arachnids have a very bad reputation. Most people think they are creepy and dangerous animals. Indeed, arachnophobia, or fear of spiders, is a common phobia (an exaggerated fear) suffered by many people. It is true that a few spiders and scorpions are venomous enough to kill people, but most arachnids are harmless to humans. They are essential in most ecosystems, regulating the numbers of insects and other small animals, and are welcomed by farmers as they help control many pests. Many people keep exotic arachnids as pets, and, in some cultures, it is bad luck to kill a spider in the house. Scientists who study arachnids are called arachnologists. They generally study arachnids for economic, ecological, and medical reasons.

Venomous bites

Some poisonous spiders, such as the Brazilian wandering spider, and scorpions, such as the bark scorpion from North America, can kill people and domestic animals. Many arachnologists work with doctors to

▶ *This arachnologist is collecting spiders from a wheat field using a vacuum machine.*

▼ *Arachnid research can involve complex machinery. This scientist is measuring the amount of air breathed by a spider.*

develop antivenins—medicines that stop the effects of an arachnid's venom. Scientists do this by milking the most dangerous spiders and scorpions by collecting samples of their venom from their fangs or stingers. Doctors may also use some venoms as anesthetics (pain-reducing drugs) and other medicines.

Arachnologists can also help save lives by understanding where and how harmful arachnids live. This knowledge can also be helpful for tackling arachnids, such as certain species of ticks, that spread disease-causing organisms to humans, and for dealing with mites that feed on stored foods or damage crops.

Types of arachnids

Many arachnologists study spiders and their cousins because they want to know more about them. The name *arachnid* comes from the Greek word *arachne*, meaning "spider," but the group also includes scorpions, ticks, mites, and harvestmen, as well as some less familiar animals, such as sun spiders and whip scorpions. All arachnids have eight legs. Most eat liquid food and many kill their prey with venom.

Spiders are the largest group of arachnids, with at least 35,000 species. With around 2,000 species, there are far fewer scorpions. The 4,500 species of harvest-

men look a little like spiders with long, spindly legs, but they cannot make silk. There are at least 30,000 tick and mite species. These animals are smaller than most other arachnids; many suck the blood of larger animals, such as birds and mammals.

Spider technology

Spiders use silk for many tasks, such as creating webs and sacs, tying up captured prey, and making shelters for themselves and their young. Arachnologists have discovered that spiders can make several types of silk of different thicknesses, strengths, and stickiness, depending on its intended use. Engineers have discovered that some silks are stronger than steel.

Scientists are studying how spiders make silk because they hope to be able to make large amounts of artificial silk. This silk could be used to make new ligaments for injured people or protective armor for soldiers.

Recently, scientists have looked into using spiders to test for drugs such as caffeine, marijuana, and benzedrine. Each drug affects the way that the spiders spin their webs. Scientists think that the degree of disruption to the web could be used as a reliable measure of the amount of drug in a sample.

ARMY ANT

A single army ant is small and harmless enough, but a swarm of these ants can kill a larger animal in its way and will leave a trail of devastation through the rain forest.

There are about 250 species of army ants living worldwide. About 150 of these species live in the Americas and the rest are found in Australia and Africa. The most studied species of army ant is the South American army ant, which ranges from southern Mexico across tropical South America.

Different ants in the colony

South American army ants are large and powerful ants, up to 1 inch (2.5 cm) long. Each colony consists of a single queen with as many as 700,000 daughters divided into two types, or castes. Members of the soldier caste are large with an orange-red head, a black body, and a red patch on the tip of the abdomen. The soldiers use their long, powerful mouthparts to defend the colony from threats, such as spiders and other colonies of ants.

Workers make up the second army ant caste. They are about half the size of the soldiers, lack the orange and red markings, and have shorter mouthparts. Workers carry out all the tasks essential to the success of the colony, such as finding food, caring for the larvae, and attending to the queen.

Unlike most other ants, army ants do not have a permanent nest and spend their time wandering from place to place. Another important task for the workers, therefore, is to carry the larvae when the ant colony is on the march.

▼ *A soldier army ant guards the colony. Its large mandibles (mouthparts) are used for fighting, not foraging.*

A nomadic lifestyle

An army ant colony is on the move most of the time. At the start of the day, hunting parties set out to find food. While most of the ants from the colony are hunting, the rest stay behind to take care of the queen and her brood. The hunters return at dusk, often having stripped the surrounding area of food, and the entire colony moves to a new site.

During this migration, the queen is sheltered in the center of the mass of ants. Often, she is almost invisible under the workers, who constantly attend her, cleaning and grooming her body. Other workers carry the brood, while the soldiers travel on the edges of the colony, ready to defend their sisters and mother from attack if necessary.

At nightfall, the colony settles into an arrangement known as a bivouac (temporary nest). The workers link themselves together with strong, hooked claws, forming a many-layered net that surrounds the colony, protecting the queen and larvae in the center. Bivouacs can be up to 3 feet (1 m) in diameter and weigh almost 2 pounds

DISTRIBUTION

SOUTH AMERICAN ARMY ANT

(1 kg). Inside the bivouac, the army ant colony produces a distinctive odor, created by the chemical signals used for communication between the members of the colony. Apart from the queen ant, all the members of a colony are unable

▼ An army ant bivouac. The ants cling to each other, making a solid mass that often hangs close to the ground between tree trunks or branches.

◀ *A group of foraging army ants holds down a trapped katydid as other ants arrive to cut up the prey.*

KEY FACTS

Name
South American army ant
(*Eciton burchelli*)

Distinctive features
Soldier is large with orange-red head and long mouthparts

Habitat
Rain forest

Behavior
Feed in fan-shaped swarms while in nomadic phase; form bivouac of bodies at night

Breeding
Queen mates once; produces daughters every six weeks during stationary phase; royal brood, with 5 or 6 queens and 3,000 winged males is produced every year

Food
Insects, spiders, scorpions, injured birds, even tethered mammals

to see, so this form of communication is very important to the smooth running of the army ant colony.

Ant raiders

Army ants look for food by swarm raiding. This involves workers moving out from the colony in search of food in a fan-shaped swarm. The front edge of the swarm can be up to 50 feet (15 m) across and can move forward at 60 feet (18 m) per hour. Workers at the front mark the way with chemicals, and the others follow this trail. The soldiers travel along the sides of the swarm.

Army ants are carnivorous (meat-eating). They prey on anything that falls in their path and is not fast enough to get away. This includes insects, spiders, small mammals, snakes, and even larger injured birds or tethered domestic animals. When an army ant worker finds an item of prey, she sends out a chemical signal that attracts others, who come to help. The ants sting their victim to death and carry it back to the colony. If the prey is too big to be easily moved, the ants cut it into small pieces with

their mouthparts. Back at the colony, the workers chew up the food, before feeding it to the larvae.

Stop and start

After about two weeks of foraging, the colony changes from its wandering way of life to a stationary one. At this time, the queen is heavily swollen with eggs and has great difficulty moving.

When the colony has settled, often in an old nest of another species of ant or a hollow log, the queen lays up to 300,000 eggs. The workers collect the eggs and look after them, keeping them clean and free of parasites. At about the same time, the larvae that hatched from the last batch of eggs pupate. Soon after, the eggs hatch, the new workers emerge from their pupae, and the colony is ready to move on again.

New colonies

Like many other insects that live in groups, the queen army ant can control the sex of her offspring by whether or not her eggs are fertilized. Fertilized eggs become females, and unfertilized

► *A mass of worker army ants covers the colony's queen and larvae. The ants cling to each other's legs.*

▼ *Army ants on the march. Workers carry the yellow pupae when the ants migrate.*

ones become males. The amount and type of food given to the female larvae dictates whether they will become workers, soldiers, or queens. For most of the year, the queen produces large broods of infertile (unable to breed) workers, but once a year she produces a "royal brood" that can reproduce.

Just five or six eggs in the royal brood are fertilized. The larvae that hatch from these eggs are fed large amounts of food, plus chemicals produced by the workers. These chemicals cause the larvae to develop into new queens. The royal brood also contains about 3,000 unfertilized eggs, which develop into males with wings.

Leaving the nest

The royal ants become adults in about three weeks. The winged males leave in search of a new colony, where—if they are accepted—they mate with a new queen before dying. The colony's own new queens are wingless and stay in the nest until the next migration.

As the colony prepares to move, some of the workers remain loyal to the old queen, but others form an attachment with one of the new queens. The old queen moves on with her army. Most of the remaining workers ally themselves to one particular new queen, who then moves away with her band of followers. Soon, males from other colonies fly in. After mating with one of them, the queen begins her life as head of a new colony. The remaining new queens do not have enough workers to forage for food or defend the colony successfully, and they soon die.

ARTHROPOD

Arthropods are a huge group of animals including spiders and other arachnids, as well as insects. Crustaceans, such as crabs, are also arthropods, as are millepedes and centipedes.

The arthropods are by far the most abundant and widespread group of animals on Earth, comprising around 90 percent of all species. Some arthropods, such as the butterflies, bees, and spiders, are very familiar. Mosquitoes and biting flies are also well known because they are pests to humans and animals, often spreading diseases. However, there are many other kinds of arthropods, some of which are too small to see. Nearly one million arthropod species have been identified by scientists, and there are new ones being discovered all the time. Arthropods live in almost every habitat on Earth, on land, in fresh water, and in salt water. Many arthropods live beneath the polar ice caps, as well as around warm volcanic vents thousands of feet below the surface of the ocean. At the other extreme, jumping spiders and springtails have been found on the summits of the tallest mountains.

▼ *This is an amphipod, a type of crustacean. It looks something like a pill bug, to which it is related. However, pill bugs live on land, while this species lives 10,000 feet (3,000 m) beneath the surface of the ocean.*

Trilobite lifestyles

Trilobites dominated the oceans for at least 300 million years and were extremely varied, with at least 15,000 known species. Some trilobites had huge compound eyes, similar to those of insects, and actively swam through the sea. Often, these trilobites had streamlined bodies. Most, however, burrowed through the mud at the bottom of the ocean. These trilobites were flattened, with reduced eyes, although some had eyes on stalks to peer above the mud. There was even a group of tiny eyeless trilobites that lived as plankton.

Many trilobites scavenged for food, but some fed on worms and other invertebrates. They protected themselves from predators by rolling into a ball; grooves on the body allowed water to flow over the gills while in this position. Like all arthropods, these animals had to molt to grow, and their bodies had clear suture lines (where the exoskeleton split.) Trilobites are commonly found as fossils, and their tracks through layers of ancient mud have also been preserved.

KEY WORDS

Arachnids
Arthropods with eight legs, including spiders and scorpions

Arthropods
Large group of animals with segmented bodies, jointed legs, and external skeletons

Crustaceans
Large group of mostly marine arthropods with two pairs of antennae, including crabs and pill bugs

Insects
The most successful group of arthropods; have six legs; most have wings and can fly

▶ *Fossil trilobites found in Utah. Trilobites are the only major group of arthropods to have become extinct.*

What is an arthropod?

Despite their incredible variety, arthropods all share certain characteristics in body plan. Unlike vertebrates, which have internal bones, arthropods support their bodies with an external skeleton. Struts and ridges from this framework, called an exoskeleton or cuticle, jut inward into the body, and the muscles attach to these struts. The exoskeleton also lines the gut and breathing systems. Arthropod bodies are divided into segments, each of which may have one or more pairs of legs.

The hard cuticle has joints in it, which allow the animal to flex and move. This is another arthropod characteristic, and from it the group derives its name (*arthropod* means "jointed feet" in Latin). Over the course of millions of years of evolution, the basic arthropod body plan has adapted to suit a great variety of different environments. This adaptability has been responsible for the success of the group. The various body segments have become specialized to perform a great variety of functions, including feeding, touch, movement, and reproduction.

Arthropod appendages

The jointed appendages of arthropods have evolved in many different ways. For example, an arachnid's front two pairs of appendages have evolved into mouthparts. One pair became pedipalps, which are used to taste food and also to transfer sperm during reproduction in some groups. The other pair has evolved into chelicerae, which are used to crush food, and they sometimes bear a set of fangs. A similar modification has occurred in the centipedes, which form part of an important arthropod group, the myriapods. Here, the front legs are modified into fangs, complete with a venom gland to paralyze prey.

Other myriapods, such as the millipedes, do not have fangs and feed on plants or decaying matter instead of other animals. The group also includes some less familiar animals, the symphyla and pauropoda, which can be extremely numerous in damp soil and rotting vegetation around the world.

Pincers and fans

Crustaceans are arthropods, most of which live under water. These animals always have two pairs of antennae. Many of the more familiar crustaceans, such as crabs, lobsters, and shrimps, have modified front legs that form pincers. Possibly the most extreme leg adaptation is seen in the barnacles. These crustaceans are covered with hard plates, and they cement their heads onto rocks and other underwater objects, such as boats, floating logs, and even the bodies of whales. Their legs are modified into a series of feathery fans, which are used to trap tiny animals and other particles in the water current.

Other arthropods

Although most crustaceans live in the ocean, there are many freshwater crustaceans, such as water fleas, as well as some land-living species, including the pill bugs. Three arthropod groups, however, live under the sea and nowhere else. The sea spiders are strange-looking animals with long, spindly legs. These animals feed on sponges, soft corals, and anenomes, often at great depths. Male sea spiders have an extra pair of legs. These are used to hold fertilized eggs until they hatch.

Horseshoe crabs burrow in the mud on the sea bottom, feeding on worms and other soft-bodied animals. These arthropods come onto beaches to mate and lay eggs. They are an ancient

group and have remained relatively unchanged for hundreds of millions of years, although today there are just five species, four in the oceans around eastern Asia and one from the Atlantic coast of North America. The last group of ocean-living arthropods were the extinct trilobites.

▲ *A scorpion with its stinger raised. Scorpions and other arachnids are arthropods.*

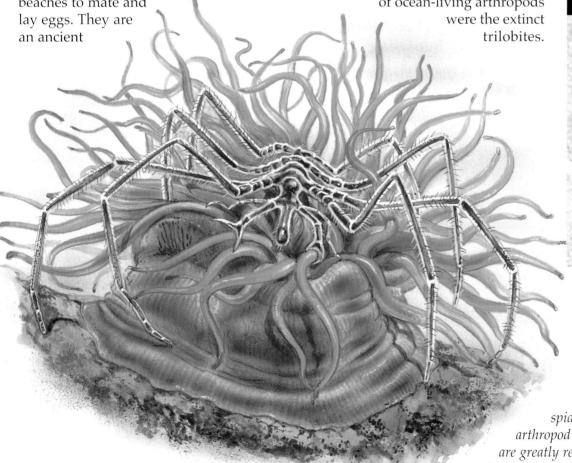

KEY WORDS

Myriapods
Many-legged terrestrial arthropods, including millipedes and centipedes

Trilobites
A large group of extinct arthropods that once lived in the ocean; often found as fossils in rocks made from mud and sand

◀ *A sea spider attacking a sea anemone. The sea spiders form their own arthropod order. Their bodies are greatly reduced, and the gut and other internal organs are located within the long, spindly legs.*

legs, with other appendages used for feeding or sensing the surroundings. Insects, the most numerous and successful of all animals, are hexapods. There are, however, three groups of noninsect hexapods. These include the Protura, tiny animals that live in soil and leaf litter, which use their front legs as sensory organs, walking on just four legs. Diplurans are also found in soil, and they have long antennae and cerci (prongs) on the abdomen. The largest group of noninsect hexapods, however, are the springtails, which live in vast numbers in damp places such as decaying wood and leaf litter, or on the surfaces of ditches and puddles.

A protective covering

The exoskeleton is made of a number of layers, some of which contain a compound called chitin. Chitin is made of long protein molecules combined with carbohydrates. It can be soft or tough; softer chitin is found in the joints of arthropod exoskeletons, while the rest is hard. This makes the exoskeleton both flexible and strong.

▲ *A spider crab foraging on coral. These animals are crabs, not spiders. They are named for their spiderlike appearance. By contrast, crab spiders live on land and walk a little like a crab.*

Trilobites were once very common, but these animals disappeared around 360 million years ago.

Insects and their relatives

The largest group of arthropods are the Hexapoda. These animals all have six

Tough plates shield the body. They are unfused, so the animal is very flexible.

long antenna

▶ *A symphylan feeds on decaying plant matter in soil. To mate, male symphylans deposit a package of sperm on the ground. The female uses her mouthparts to place the package into a pocket inside the mouth. Later, she transfers it to her reproductive organs.*

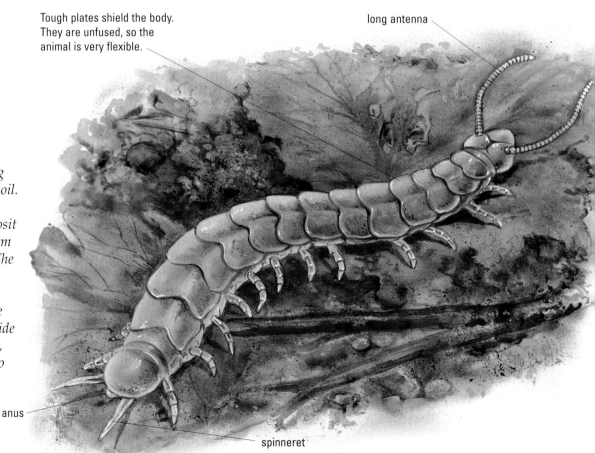

anus

spinneret

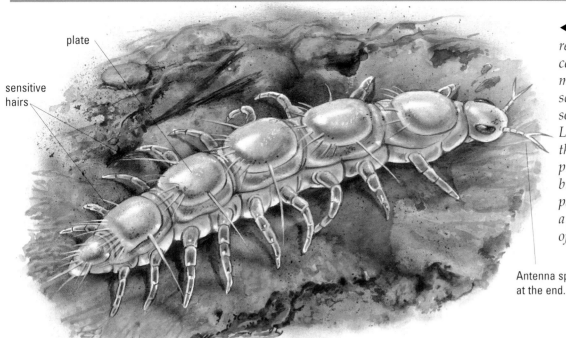

plate

sensitive hairs

◀ Pauropods are related to the centipedes and millipedes. They scavenge for food in soil or leaf litter. Like symphylans, their bodies are protected by plates, but those of pauropods cover a fused pair of segments.

Antenna splits at the end.

The exoskeleton is crucial to arthropods in a number of ways. It protects them from damage and from attack by predators or parasites. It also serves as a solid attachment point for muscles, allowing activities such as flying, running, and jumping.

The exoskeleton also helps prevent water loss. Small animals lose water much more quickly than larger ones. Animals without a waterproof covering are limited to living in damp areas, such as wetlands and rain forests. The arthropods' exoskeleton allows them to live in drier habitats, since it forms a barrier between the water-filled internal organs and the outside environment. This, plus the ability of some (such as insects) to close their spiracles (air holes), has allowed these animals to move into new habitats and is probably the main reason that insects are such a successful group of animals.

Saving water is most important in desert environments. Some desert beetles collect water that condenses on their bodies in the form of droplets. Others cannot fly, because their hard outer wings have become fused to the body to keep as much water in as possible, while the inner wings have completely disappeared.

The exoskeleton is rigid and does not stretch. So, in order to grow, arthropods must shed the exoskeleton, expand quickly, and then grow a new covering. This process is called molting. Molting involves shedding the entire cuticle, including the insides of the gut and respiratory systems.

The importance of arthropods

Arthropods exist in such huge numbers and diversity that it is no surprise that they are an essential part of the cycle of life in all habitats. Some feed on detritus (rotting material), others feed on other

▼ This pill bug has tough plates on its body to keep it from drying out. Other land crustaceans include land crabs and shore-dwelling amphipods.

The earliest arthropods

Arthropods appeared around 600 million years ago. They diversified quickly during a period known as the Cambrian explosion, around 520 million years ago. In addition to a number of bizarre animals unrelated to any others, many unusual arthropods from this time have been found in a Canadian deposit known as the Burgess shale.

The animals lived on a reef but were swept suddenly into deeper water by a mud slide, which preserved the soft parts of their bodies. As well as many trilobites, arthropods from the Burgess shale include *Anomalocaris*, a large predator with long feelers on its head and a mouth shaped like a pineapple ring. *Marella* swam using its feathery gills. *Opabinia* had five eyes, with a grasping arm reaching from its head, while *Leanchoilia* used long whiplike appendages rather than eyes to find its way. Most of these strange arthropods disappeared soon after the Cambrian explosion, leaving the trilobites and ancestors of recent arthropods to evolve and dominate the ancient seas.

SEE ALSO

- *Centipede*
- *False scorpion*
- *Millipede*
- *Pill bug*
- *Primitive insect*
- *Scorpion*
- *Spider*
- *Sun spider*
- *Tick and mite*
- *Whip scorpion*

arthropods, and some feed on plants or fungi. Feeding animals convert their food into proteins that are used to build up their bodies. In turn, many vertebrates benefit by eating arthropods. At up to 110 tons (100 tonnes), the blue whale is the largest animal known ever to have existed on Earth. It feeds only on schools of tiny shrimplike crustaceans, called krill, which it extracts in huge numbers from the water using its massive sievelike mouth.

Recycling nutrients

Arthropods in the soil carry out an important job by helping break down dead vegetation and animals on the forest floor. This releases the nutrients back into the soil, allowing them to become part of the new growth of trees, and indirectly, of herbivorous and predatory animals.

In woodlands, ants, termites, and other burrowing insects help turn the soil over, allowing oxygen to enter into the soil. Arthropods, mostly insects, are responsible for the pollination of almost all of the flowering plants in the world. Without insects, the plants would not be able to pollinate, and new plants would never be produced.

▶ *Mating horseshoe crabs on a New Jersey beach. These large arthropods are not true crabs but are classified within their own class. They live on the ocean floor, feeding on mollusks and worms as they burrow through the mud. However, they come on land to reproduce.*

ASSASSIN BUG

These bugs are expert killers and are well camouflaged to hide from their prey. Some species spread diseases to people.

The 6,000 species of assassin bugs are named for the way some of them stalk their quarry and then strike with a daggerlike beak, called a rostrum. After feeding, the bug folds the rostrum into a groove on the underside of the thorax (midbody). Assassin bugs communicate with sound. This is produced by scraping the rostrum along this groove.

Catching prey

Many assassin bugs are masters of disguise, able to blend in with their surroundings. This allows them to stalk their prey without being spotted. Most are brown or black, although some tropical forms are brightly colored and hide in flowers.

Some attract insects by releasing a smelly chemical, but most are active hunters, sometimes taking to the wing to hunt down their quarry. Many of these bugs grip prey with their spiny front legs. Some have pads on their legs, covered with hairs. These hairs help the bug hold on to prey by secreting sticky chemicals. A few species boost the stickiness of the front legs by smearing them with resin (sap) collected from plants.

Small assassin bugs feed on mosquitoes and other small types of flies. Larger species can reach up to 1.5 inches (38 mm) long and are able to tackle millipedes and large beetles.

Like other bugs, assassin bugs have piercing, sucking mouthparts. They insert the rostrum into the area between the head and thorax and inject saliva into their prey. This paralyzes the victim before breaking down the tissues. The bug then sucks out the juices.

Feeding on a range of insects

Most assassin bugs are found on foliage in warmer countries, and some are important predators of crop pests. The wheel bug of North America is a dark brown bug, easily recognizable by the distinctive cogwheel on top of the adult's thorax.

KEY FACTS

Name
Wheel bug
(*Arilus cristatus*)

Distinctive features
Gray-brown bug with cogwheel on the thorax

Food
Wide range of small insects

Distribution
Southern United States and parts of Central America

Size
Adult: up to 1.25 inches (32 mm) long

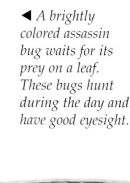

◀ *A brightly colored assassin bug waits for its prey on a leaf. These bugs hunt during the day and have good eyesight.*

As both nymph and adult, wheelbugs are very active hunters. Many of their victims are pest insects, such as sawflies, leaf bugs, and grasshoppers. However, wheel bugs also eat useful species, such as honeybees, which pollinate flowers, and ladybugs, which eat aphids.

Luring prey

Some small assassin bugs release sweet-tasting chemicals from their abdomens, on which ants feed. Unfortunately for the ants, the tasty chemicals contain a nerve toxin that paralyzes the ants as they feed. The bug, which is not affected by the poison, can then eat the ants. Several highly specialized assassin bugs steal their food rather than catch it. These long-legged bugs plunder insect food from spiderwebs. A few even prey on the spiders themselves.

Spreading disease

In Central and South America, several species of assassin bugs spread the dangerous Chagas' disease to people. The disease is caused by tiny single-celled organisms called trypanosomes. The bugs hide away during the day but emerge at night to feed on blood. They bite sleeping people, often around the mouth. Because of this, these bugs are sometimes called kissing bugs. The bugs leave excrement on the skin. The feces can contain trypanosomes, which pass into the person's body through the wound made by the bug. The trypanosomes destroy nerve and muscle tissue, especially in the heart and digestive system. This untreatable disease can cause heart failure and death.

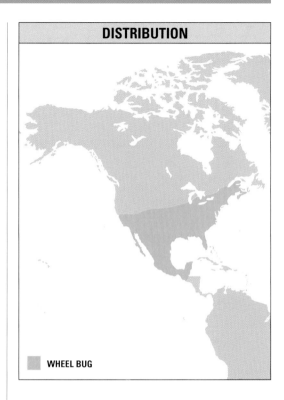

DISTRIBUTION

■ WHEEL BUG

▼ *An assassin bug lies hidden on a goldenrod flower, waiting for a bumblebee to land, before stabbing it with its long mouthparts.*

BARK BEETLE

Bark beetles are among the most destructive forest pests known. They bore tunnels through wood, and some bring fungi inside trees to feed their larvae.

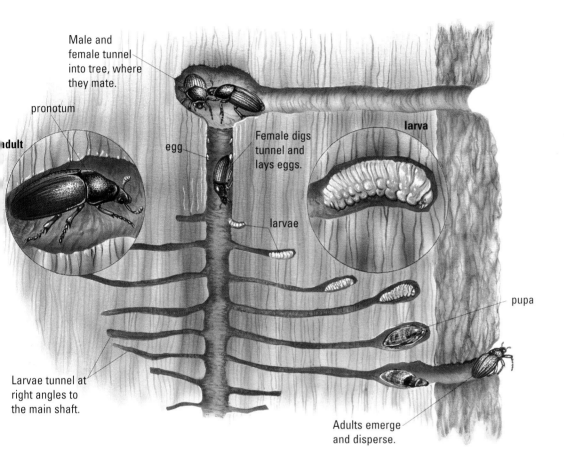

Male and female tunnel into tree, where they mate.

pronotum

adult

egg

Female digs tunnel and lays eggs.

larva

larvae

pupa

Larvae tunnel at right angles to the main shaft.

Adults emerge and disperse.

◀ The life cycle of the European elm bark beetle. Bark beetles tunnel out galleries in the wood. The pattern made by the tunnels is different for every species.

KEY FACTS

Name
European elm bark beetle (*Scolytus multistriatus*)

Distinctive features
Small, reddish-brown; backward-pointing spine on the underside of the abdomen

Habitat
Tunnels into wood in forests and parks with elm trees; introduced to North America

Food
Larva eats fungus introduced by adults; fungus causes disease in trees

Size
0.1 to 0.12 inches (2.5 to 3 mm) long

Every year, bark beetles destroy enough wood, mostly from conifers, to make 8 billion feet of planks, costing timber companies millions of dollars. There are about 6,000 species living around the world. Many tropical bark beetles live in the stemlike petioles of large leaves or mine inside the vines and lianas that hang from the forest canopy. Many species live in seeds.

Although most bark beetles are tropical, the best-known species are those from northern temperate forests. Bark beetle adults are easy to recognize by

their small, bullet-shaped bodies. These brown insects are generally less than 0.4 inches (10 mm) long. Many have ridges on their hardened elytra (wing cases) and on the shieldlike pronotum that covers the head.

Most bark beetles feed and breed under the bark. Some species gather in large numbers to attack whole forests of weakened trees. The most commercially important bark beetles attack coniferous trees such as pine and spruce. All woody parts of the tree can be attacked. Some species live in small branches or

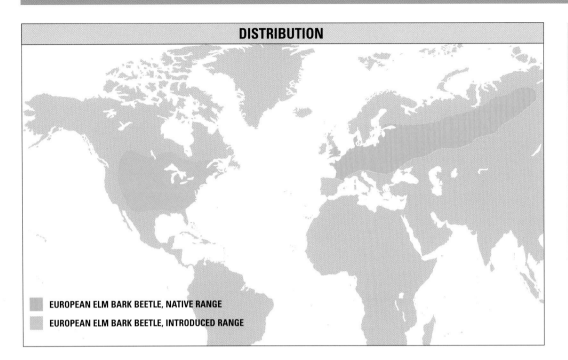

DISTRIBUTION

EUROPEAN ELM BARK BEETLE, NATIVE RANGE

EUROPEAN ELM BARK BEETLE, INTRODUCED RANGE

twigs, some only in cones, some in larger branches, and yet others in the lower parts of the trunk or the roots.

Tunnels and galleries

The first evidence of bark beetle attack is the appearance of dust around circular holes bored by the beetles. Bark beetles can be either monogamous (one male mates with one female) or polygamous (one male mates with many females). In monogamous species, the female bores the first hole and enters the tree and the male joins her later. In polygamous species, it is the male that enters first, followed by his harem of females.

Once inside, the adults make a series of tunnels in the wood. Eggs are laid along the tunnels, and after hatching, the larvae bore into nearby wood. They feed on the wood for some time and eventually pupate at the end of the tunnels. When the adults emerge, they bore through the bark and disperse.

Partnerships with fungi

Ambrosia beetles get their common name from the ambrosia fungus that they carry in pockets on their bodies. The beetles infect trees with the fungus. Ambrosia beetle larvae bore deep into the wood rather than just under the bark. The fungus is carried by the adults and is spread inside the tunnels just before the eggs are laid. The larvae then feed on the fungus that grows on the walls of the tunnels. If the fungus grows too quickly, it clogs up the tunnels and kills the larvae. For this reason, the adult beetles usually stay with their young and help keep the fungus under control.

Fungi introduced by beetles can kill the tree. Many woodlands have been blighted by Dutch elm disease, which is caused by a beetle-carried fungus.

▼ *This is an engraver beetle. These small beetles cause a great deal of damage to firs and spruces throughout North America. They get their name from the characteristic patterns they leave as they tunnel through the wood.*

BEDBUG

Feeding on the blood of their sleeping hosts, these bugs are common in bedrooms, as well as the roosts of wild animals. Their bites cause a rash, but they do not pass on diseases.

As adults, bedbugs are tiny, at just 0.12 to 0.25 inches (3 to 6 mm) long. They have tiny wings and cannot fly. The bugs' flattened shape enables them to hide in narrow crevices. They use their antennae to detect the heat and carbon dioxide emitted by the hosts on which they feed.

Like other bugs, these insects have piercing mouthparts used for sucking liquids. These include sawblade-shaped stylets that anchor into the skin. The mouthparts also include two tubes. One injects saliva into the host. The saliva contains anticoagulants, which stop the blood from clotting (hardening) so it can be sucked up through the second tube. The bug withdraws the mouthparts into a sheath when they are not in use.

Feeding on humans

Many different kinds of bedbugs live in the roosts and nests of bats and birds and feed on these animals. However, at least three types of bedbugs have a taste for human blood: the tropical bedbug,

▼ *A scanning electron microscope image of a bedbug. The mouthparts are long and pointed, allowing the bug to pierce the skin of the host.*

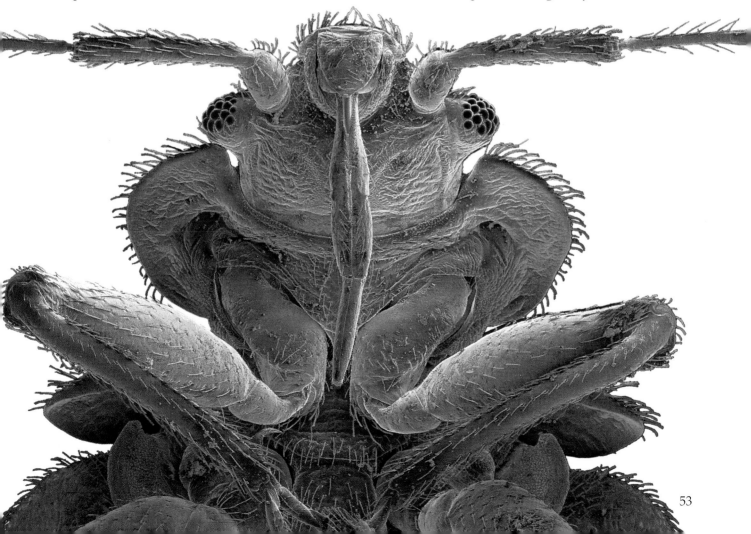

the west African bedbug, and the human bedbug. These insects feed on many types of warm-blooded animals. For example, the human bedbug feeds on birds and bats, as well as people.

Fertilization and egg laying

Bedbugs are unusual because during mating, the male does not fertilize the female's eggs by inserting his sperm into a genital opening. Instead, the male cuts a hole in her body and sheds his sperm into her body fluids. This process is called traumatic insemination. The sperm cells travel through the female's hemolymph (blood) and then fertilize the insect's eggs when they arrive in her reproductive system.

The female lays three or four eggs each day, or more if conditions are right, until she has laid about 100 eggs in all. The eggs hatch into the first nymph (juvenile) stage after three weeks or so.

After hatching, young bedbugs look very similar to the adults. Before growing into an adult, the nymphs molt (shed their skin) a total of five times.

Like the adults, they feed on the blood of warm-blooded animals, and they must feed before molting.

In the right conditions, such as in a house with a warm bedroom, bedbugs can complete their life cycle in three months. In cooler environments, or where hosts are scarce, the bedbug may starve for many months and take more than a year to complete its life cycle.

Hiding away

The adults and nymphs hide away in cracks in wooden bed frames, along the edges of mattresses, and even behind peeling wallpaper. They come out to feed in the early hours of the morning, or during dull, overcast days. They take just five to ten minutes to consume all the blood they need.

Bedbugs can quickly increase in numbers. In severe infestations, their waste creates a distinctive, pungent smell. Animals can sometimes harbor very large numbers; around 1,800 Mexican chicken bugs have been found on a single barn owl.

KEY FACTS

Name
Human bedbug
(*Cimex lectularius*)

Distinctive features
Flattened, oval body; reddish-brown when unfed, darker after feeding

Habitat
Bedrooms, or the roosts and nests of birds and bats

Food
Blood of people, birds, or bats

Breeding
Male deposits sperm in a hole cut into the body of the female; female lays around 100 eggs

Distribution
Lives all around the world

Size
Adult: 0.12 inches (3 mm) unfed; 0.25 inches (6 mm) fed

◀ *A human bedbug feeding. These insects increase greatly in size when they feed and change color due to the presence of hemoglobin (a blood pigment) in their stomachs.*

A change of food source

Scientists believe that human bedbugs were once parasites of birds and bats. When human ancestors began living in the same places as roosting animals, such as caves, the bugs took this opportunity to feed on a new host. As people began to build homes, the bugs were taken along by accident.

Bedbugs transmit surprisingly few infections to the humans on which they feed. Although bedbugs are able to host several disease-causing organisms in laboratory experiments, they do not seem to pass these diseases on to humans. This may be because the insects have only recently switched from feeding on bats and birds to sucking human blood in the last 500,000 years. Perhaps human disease-causing organisms have yet to evolve a way of transferring from the stomach of the bedbug to the salivary glands, from

▲ *A bedbug moving over bedclothes. The oval, flattened shape allows these insects to hide in tiny cracks and crevices near the place where the host sleeps.*

SEE ALSO

- *Bug*
- *Feeding*
- *Larva, nymph, and pupa*
- *Pest*

where the organisms could infect other people when the bedbug bites. For many people, the worst that can happen is a rash where the bugs have bitten, and a bad night's sleep. A few people react allergically to the saliva injected by the bug during the bite, and a painful, itching swelling results. After repeated bites, a person can become sensitized to the saliva.

Removing an infestation

Once a house has become infested, bedbugs can be difficult to find and remove, since they are able to hide away in very small spaces. All bedding needs to be cleaned and disinfected, and insecticides must be applied carefully to remove the bugs from every nook and crevice. Due to improvements in hygiene, bedbugs are less common today than they were 50 years ago, but they are still widespread.

BEE

Bees are distinctive insects, with many species covered in thick striped fur. Most bees are solitary, but a few species live in social colonies, defending their nests with powerful stingers.

What do you think of when you imagine a bee? Probably, you imagine a hive of hardworking honeybees, all busy collecting nectar from flowers or stinging their enemies to defend the queen and the rest of their nestmates. The reason honeybees are so well known is that they have been extremely valuable to humans for a very long time. These insects have been kept in beehives for thousands of years, used to pollinate crops and to provide people with honey and beeswax. However, these few species are not representative of the whole group, many of which have a very different lifestyle from that of the group-living honeybees.

Bees are related to the ants, wasps, and sawflies. There are around 20,000 species of bees, which are classified in

◀ *A leaf-cutting bee returns to its nest with a piece of a leaf. These bees line their nests with fragments of leaves.*

DISTRIBUTION

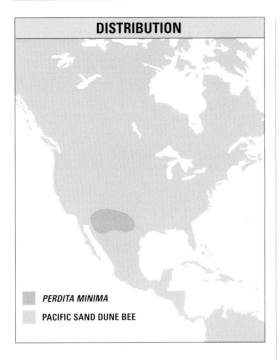

- PERDITA MINIMA
- PACIFIC SAND DUNE BEE

six main groups. Of these, only about 800 species live in social groups. These include the honeybees, bumblebees, stingless bees, and sweat bees.

Living in colonies

Social bees live in colonies, the largest of which may contain as many as 80,000 individuals. These societies are made up mainly of females called workers, all of which are the daughters of a single queen, who spends her time laying hundreds or thousands of eggs every day. The workers perform all the jobs necessary to keep the society going,

such as collecting food, repairing the nest, and fending off attackers. A small proportion of the bees in a social colony are males, or drones. The drones are produced so they can mate with queens from other colonies. They have no other task to perform for the colony.

Solitary bees

The other 19,200 or so bee species live alone. In these species, single females make nests in which to lay their eggs. They do not take care of their offspring after they have hatched.

Unlike social bees, solitary bees do not specialize in different tasks at different stages of their life but do everything for themselves. Solitary bees include the carpenter bees, digger bees, mason bees, leaf-cutting bees, plasterer bees, and some of the sweat bees. Many solitary bees make their homes close together in the same area, or even in separate chambers off a shared space, but they do not cooperate in building their nests, finding food, or feeding their offspring in the way that social bees do.

Parasitic bees

Cuckoo bees are solitary, but they are parasites of social bees. A parasite is an animal that takes advantage of another host animal. Like the birds of the same name, cuckoo bees lay their eggs in the colonies of other bee species, where

▼ *Scientists study honeybees on a honeycomb from an artificial hive. Beekeepers use smoke to divert bees' attention. Bees respond to smoke, a sign of fire, by gorging on honey and preparing to abandon the nest.*

Associations with mites

Many bees have parasitic mites on their bodies. These tiny arachnids suck hemolymph (blood) from their hosts. However, not all mites are enemies of bees. Some are even carried by new queens. Before the new queens leave their mother's nest, the mites climb onto them and cling on until they arrive in a new nest, where they get off the queen and begin eating their host's trash, keeping her nest clean. Some carpenter bees have an even closer relationship with mites. The females have pouches on their abdomens in which they carry mites. The mites lay eggs on the bee's larvae, and the young nymphs keep the larvae free of fungi.

▲ *Stingless bees at the entrance of their nest. Like honeybees, these bees are pollen and nectar feeders and store honey in a honeycomb. However, unlike honeybees, these bees are unable to use their small stingers.*

Defense without stingers

Most of the social bees have stingers. The bees respond to threats to the nest in a group, driving away intruders. Although they have tiny stingers, stingless bees are unable to use them, and they must use alternative defensive methods. These bees coat the entrance to their nest in sticky resin. Predatory insects are unable to get very far past the entrance.

Many bees can inflict a painful bite with their mandibles; in addition, some stingless bees are able to secrete an irritating chemical from glands into the wound. The chemical causes intense burning pain and leads to painful blisters. Not surprisingly, these insects are also called fire bees.

their nest in a part of the body known as the honey stomach and then deposit it in wax cells. Over time, water evaporates from the nectar. Sometimes, this process is accelerated when the bees flap their wings over the liquid. This turns the nectar into honey, on which the bees feed. During its lifetime, a honeybee worker brings enough nectar back to its colony to make as much as 0.1 pounds (45 grams) of honey.

Pollen feeders

Most bees, however, feed on pollen, which is rich in protein. The pollen clings to tiny branched hairs that cover the bee's body. Honeybees and bumblebees are more specialized pollen collectors. These bees have "pollen baskets" on their hind legs, into which they pack pollen as they forage.

Many bees are able to collect pollen from a wide variety of different plants, but a few bees are very selective in the flowers they visit. For example, *Protanendra* bees from the deserts of southwestern North America visit only the vibrant purple blossoms of silverleaf nightshade plants.

Bees are important pollinators of flowering plants. As they forage, some of the pollen from one flower rubs onto the reproductive parts of other flowers of the same species, fertilizing them.

their offspring are raised by the host workers. Some parasitic species lay their eggs in the nests of other solitary bees, where the larvae feed on food intended for the hosts' larvae.

Visiting flowers for food

Social or solitary, one thing most bees have in common is the type of food they eat. Unlike wasps and many ants, almost all bees are plant eaters, and they are often seen collecting food from flowering plants. Some social bees drink a sweet, sugary liquid called nectar from the flowers, using a long, strawlike proboscis. They carry the nectar back to

Some stingless bees do not waste time collecting their own pollen from flowers, but invade the colonies of other bees and steal their food supplies. This group of bees also includes the only meat-eating species, which feeds on carrion (flesh of dead animals) to get its protein. Sweat bees are so called because they have a habit of licking sweat from animals and people. The bee gets important mineral salts in this way.

Stinging defense

Bees can give a painful sting if they feel threatened. At the end of their abdomens, female bees have a sharp stinger connected to a gland that pumps poison into the wound. The stinger has tiny hooks on it, which catch in the victim's skin and pull the sting out of the bee's body, killing the bee. Social bees are much more likely to sting attackers than solitary bees. Only the queen social bee reproduces, but each worker bee is the sister of the queen's offspring. Honeybees sacrifice their lives in the defense of the colony. The

◀ *This Osmia bee is a pollinator of blueberries and is of great benefit to farmers of these fruits. Bees are responsible for pollinating crops worth billions of dollars every year.*

▼ *A cross section through the nest of a solitary tropical mining bee, showing development from egg to adult.*

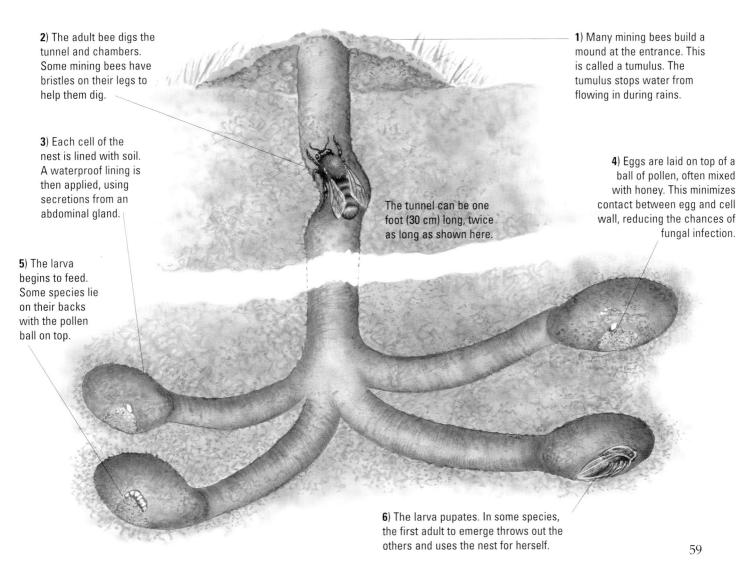

2) The adult bee digs the tunnel and chambers. Some mining bees have bristles on their legs to help them dig.

3) Each cell of the nest is lined with soil. A waterproof lining is then applied, using secretions from an abdominal gland.

5) The larva begins to feed. Some species lie on their backs with the pollen ball on top.

The tunnel can be one foot (30 cm) long, twice as long as shown here.

1) Many mining bees build a mound at the entrance. This is called a tumulus. The tumulus stops water from flowing in during rains.

4) Eggs are laid on top of a ball of pollen, often mixed with honey. This minimizes contact between egg and cell wall, reducing the chances of fungal infection.

6) The larva pupates. In some species, the first adult to emerge throws out the others and uses the nest for herself.

Buzzing for food

Many flowers attract bees by providing nectar. The anthers (pollen-producing organs) of these flowers are usually easily accessed by insects. However, the anthers of some plants are long, narrow tubes with holes at one end. These plants do not provide nectar because they have a close relationship with bees such as bumblebees, which eat only pollen and pollinate the plants as they go from one to another.

To get the pollen to drop down from the anthers, the bees vibrate their flight muscles powerfully. The buzzing sends vibrations through the flower, and the pollen, which is typically much finer than in other plants, is shaken free from the anther by the vibrations. The bee collects the pollen and flies away to another plant, or back to the nest, where the pollen is stored away before being eaten by the young. This process is called buzz pollination, and it is of great importance for crops such as tomatoes and eggplants.

stinging bee will die, but its relatives will benefit should the enemy be driven off. Solitary bees do not have hordes of sisters ready to defend their young and instead tend to try to escape to fight another day. Despite their name, stingless bees do have a small sting, but they defend themselves by biting with their sharp mouthparts.

Even social bees are generally not aggressive, and they will not sting unless they feel that they or the colony are in danger. One exception is the Africanized bee, which is quick to attack its enemies in large numbers, sometimes stinging them to death. This bee is the product of hybridization (crossing) experiments in Brazil between African honeybees and local Brazilian honeybees. The Africanized hybrids became established in the wild in 1957, and were very successful.

▶ *A digger bee emerging from its burrow. These bees are solitary and are common throughout North America. Digger bees feed on pollen from just one or two types of flowers.*

▼ *A green metallic bee. This bee hides by blending in with the drops of dew that cover rain forests.*

digger bees excavate holes in the ground. Similarly, the Pacific sand dune bee digs its nests in the hard, compacted sand of dunes on the west coast of the United States. Leaf-cutting bees get their name because they cut circles from leaves with their slicing mandibles (mouthparts) and use the leaf pieces to line their nests. Other solitary bees line their nest chambers using secretions from a gland in the abdomen.

The bee life cycle

Like ants and wasps, bees are insects that undergo complete metamorphosis. There are four stages to their life cycle: egg, larva, pupa, and adult. The bees at each of these stages look very different from those at other stages.

In most social colonies, the eggs and larvae are kept in wax compartments called brood cells. Bumblebees, honeybees, and other social species have nurses that take care of the larvae and feed them as they develop, but solitary species such as sweat bees and carpenter bees do not stay around long enough to see their offspring grow. Instead, they leave balls of pollen behind in the nesting cells when they lay their eggs, so that the larvae will have food when they hatch. This behavior is known as provisioning. In some solitary bees such as carpenter bees, the pollen balls are stuck to the nest walls, and the eggs are laid in a cluster at the bottom of the nest, which is often located in a hollow plant stem.

Adult bees come in a great range of sizes. Wallace's lost bee from Indonesia is the largest known species. Its body measures up to 1.6 inches (4 cm) long, and the wings can be 2.5 inches (6.3 cm) across. This species digs brood chambers inside the nests of termites. By contrast, some bees are tiny; the stingless *Perdita minima* bee from central North America measures just 0.08 inches (2 mm) long.

As adults, workers in colonies and solitary bees live for just a few days to a month; social bee queens, on the other hand, may live for many years.

These bees have spread throughout South and Central America and into the southwestern United States.

Bee nests

The nests of solitary bees are much smaller and simpler than the hives built by the social bees and are usually made in hollow wood, wall crevices, or holes in the ground. A bee's common name often relates to where the insects build their nests. For example, carpenter bees dig small tunnels in wood, while many

SEE ALSO

- *Africanized bee*
- *Bee fly*
- *Bumblebee*
- *Communication*
- *Defense*
- *Honeybee*
- *Larva, nymph, and pupa*
- *Pollination*
- *Social insect*
- *Wasp*

Bee fly

The maggots of bee flies are parasites of other insect larvae, especially those species that live underground or in nests. After becoming adults, bee flies feed on flower nectar, and some look like bees or wasps.

Adult bee flies have robust, hairy bodies and long, tubular mouthparts. Bee flies get their name because some species look a little like bumblebees, although unlike these insects they do not have a stinger and have only two wings instead of four. A few species look very similar to stinging wasps, and as a result most predators give these flies a wide berth.

Parasites inside and out

Adult bee flies are nectar feeders, but their larvae feed on a variety of other insects. The larvae of most of the 4,500 species of bee flies are ectoparasites—they attach to a host and feed on hemolymph (blood) from the outside. However, a few species are endoparasites (develop and feed inside the host), and some are active hunters. Most bee fly maggots attack hosts that live in burrows and nests under the soil, especially the larvae of solitary wasps and bees. Other underground targets of bee fly maggots include the larvae of tiger beetles and ant lions, and the egg pods of grasshoppers.

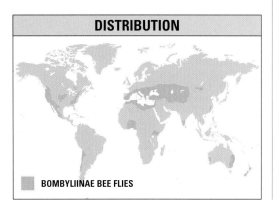

DISTRIBUTION

BOMBYLIINAE BEE FLIES

Being a fly

The life cycle of a typical fly, such as a member of the Bombyliinae subfamily, begins when a mother lays an egg in an exposed area close to the nests of hosts. The eggs of many species are coated with a protective layer of sand before being dropped to the ground.

The newly hatched larva seeks out a host, often by crawling into the host's burrow. A bee fly's later larval stages are very inactive compared to the highly mobile first stage.

▲ *A common bee fly feeding on nectar. The mouthparts of these insects form a long proboscis.*

SEE ALSO

- *Bee*
- *Fly*
- *Mimicry*
- *Wasp*

GLOSSARY

abdomen: the rear body section of insects, spiders, and other arthropods

antennae (an-TEH-nee): sensitive jointed feelers on the heads of insects

anticoagulant (AN-TY-coh-AHG-yuh-luhnt): chemical released by bloodsucking insects to stop blood from clotting

arthropod (AHR-thruh-PAHD): animal with several pairs of jointed limbs and a hard outer covering (exoskeleton)

cephalothorax (SEH-fuh-luh-THOR-AKS): the fused head and thorax of a spider

chelicerae (kih-LIH-suh-ree): appendages near an arachnid's mouth; those of spiders carry fangs

chitin (KEYE-tuhn): a tough material in the exoskeletons of arthropods

cribellum (krih-BEH-luhm): a small plate in front of the spinnerets of certain spiders that helps spin very fine silk

diffusion (dih-FYOO-zhuhn): the movement of a gas from a point of high concentration to a point of lower concentration

elytra: wing cases that protect the hind wings

enzyme: biological substance that speeds up chemical reactions inside the body

exoskeleton: the hard outer covering of an arthropod; contains chitin (KEYE-tuhn)

hemocyanin (HEE-moh-SIH-uh-nuhn): substance in the blood of spiders and other invertebrates that binds to oxygen, storing it and transporting it around the body

hemolymph (HEE-muh-LIMPF): fluid pumped around the body of an arthropod by the heart; similar to vertebrate blood

honeydew: sugary liquid released by many bugs and some caterpillars as a waste product after feeding on plant sap

hormone: chemical transported around the body by hemolymph

larva (LAR-vuh): young form of insect that looks different from the adult, lives in a different habitat (type of place), and eats different foods

microvilli (MEYE-kroh-VIH-LEYE): bumps in the wall of the gut that increase its surface area

molt: shedding of the exoskeleton by an arthropod as it grows

mutualism (MYOO-chuh-wuh-LIH-zuhm): relationship between two different species in which both parties benefit

nymph (NIHMF): young form of insect that looks very similar to the adult and usually lives in a similar habitat (type of place)

ovipositor (OH-vuh-PAH-zuh-tuhr): tube on a female insect's abdomen for laying eggs

parthenogenesis (PAR-thuh-noh-JEH-nuh-suhs): production of offspring by females without needing to mate with a male

parasite: organism that feeds on another organism called a host; the host may be damaged but is not killed by the parasite

peritrophic (PEE-ree-TROH-fihk) **envelope**: protective covering over food in an insect's gut to prevent harmful chemicals and tiny organisms from entering the body

petiole (PEH-tee-OHL): narrow waist between the thorax and abdomen of wasps and ants

pheromone (FEH-ruh-MOHN): chemical released into the air by an insect, often to attract mates or to direct other insects to food

predator: an animal that feeds by catching and killing other animals

pronotum (PROH-noh-tuhm): shieldlike covering of the first segment of the thorax

pupa (PYOO-puh): stage during which a larva transforms into an adult insect

rostrum (RAH-struhm): pointed, sucking mouthparts of a bug

sperm: male sex cell

spermatheca (SPUHR-muh-THEE-kuh): package of sperm produced by many arthropods

spinneret (SPIH-nuh-REHT): silk-spinning organ at the rear of a spider's abdomen

spiracle (SPIH-rih-kuhl): opening in the exoskeleton through which arthropods breathe

thorax: midbody section of an insect to which legs and wings are attached

trachea (TRAY-kee-uh): tube through which air travels directly to the cells inside an insect's body

INDEX

Page numbers in **bold** refer to main articles; those in *italics* refer to picture captions.